COMMERCIAL
INTERIORS

DESIGN MEDIA PUBLISHING LIMITED

© 2010 by Design Media Publishing Limited
This edition published in January 2011

Design Media Publishing Limited
20/F Manulife Tower
169 Electric Rd, North Point
Hong Kong
Tel: 00852-28672587
Fax: 00852-25050411
E-mail: Kevinchoy@designmediahk.com
www.designmediahk.com

Editing: "Commercial Interiors" Team
Proofreading: Catherine Chang
Design/Layout: Coraline Cao

ISBN 978-988-19738-2-5

Printed in China

contents

OFFICE

RESTAURANT

Contents

Paul, Hastings, Janofsky & Walker, LLP—Paris

Project Name: Paul, Hastings, Janofsky & Walker, LLP—Paris   **Designer:** Progetto CMR - Massimo Roj Architects   **Location:** Paris, France   **Photographer:** Eric Laignel   **Time:** September 2007   **Total Size:** 48,000 sf

Unique to this project, walls could not be reconfigured in the historic building, so design was focused on furniture, cabinetry and the creative use of light. Careful planning allowed for functional segregation of public reception rooms from private practice areas while respecting the historic fabric of the building. The furnishings are an eclectic combination of classic pieces with sleek custom conference tables and seating unified by a restrained palette of cream and dove gray upholstery. The color scheme includes a subtle collection of grays and beige that build upon the historic features of the building with a diverse range of texture and sheen to create visible depth. There are gilded and gold-painted walls combined with back-painted glass top tables. An endlessly spiraling staircase rises from the sunbathed lobby with built in banquette and an up-lit dome over the reception desk. The lighting design is a sophisticated blend of restored original fixtures, bespoke Murano chandeliers, concealed cove up-lighting and contemporary backlit glass elements.

The project, which included approximately 4460 square metres spread among eight floors, was designed to accommodate 134 attorneys and staff, a conference floor and prominent library. The primary materials used were limestone, artisanal plaster, limed European oak, wrought iron and glass.

Paul,Hastings,Janofsky & Walker,LLP – Los Angeles

Project Name: Paul, Hastings, Janofsky & Walker, LLP – Los Angeles
Designer: Progetto CMR - Massimo Roj Architects   **Location:** Los Angeles,USA
Photographer: Benny Chan   **Time:** 2007   **Total Size:** 194,400 sf

Paul, Hastings, Janofsky & Walker, a multi-disciplinary law firm with offices worldwide, sought a unifying design scheme for its offices that reinforces the firm's corporate identity and branding efforts and reflects the culture of one of the nation's most dynamic law firms. Each office employs the newly designed standards, yet is able to maintain the distinct personality of the individual offices.

Paul Hastings' Los Angeles headquarters were designed to endorse the culture established by the law firm's young, vibrant managing partners. The partners sought a design that would reflect their commitment to an expanding enterprise, innovative solutions, and a progressive environment.

The office environment was designed with a modern, neutral palette and angled planes of drywall that reflect and enhance natural light throughout the 190,000 square foot space. The main reception area exemplifies the design approach — the two-storey atrium space is filled with natural light and colour, providing a perfect backdrop for dramatic views of Los Angeles. The attorney offices were designed with custom, opaque glass walls and clerestories to draw natural light deeper into the space. The ethereal quality of the office design is calming and epitomizes Paul Hastings' business approach; yet, the richly textured design materials and careful detailing offer a counterpoint to the lightness of the space and reinforce the law firm's strength and depth.

Manchester Square

Project Name: Manchester Square   **Designer:** SHH   **Location:** London, UK   **Photographer:** James Silverman   **Time:** 2008

It is a new London office interiors scheme for a private company in London's west end, designed by SHH, working closely with client-side design director Zeljko Popovic. The Manchester Square offices are the result of a brief to create a "high impact, 21st century office interior with a strong personality" with more in common with a gentlemen's club than a traditional office space. The requisite air of subtlety and elegance in the scheme is reflected in the complete lack of external branding at the company's front door.

Although the property was made up of a classic (and Grade II-listed) Georgian townhouse with a former stables and garage mews building to the rear, the client was very open to a sense of contrast for the scheme, favouring a highly contemporary treatment. The inherited interior — also previously an office — was not particularly grand, but any standout details were to be retained (such as marble mosaic floor tiles in the entrance area, a number of marble-inlaid fireplaces and highly detailed ceiling cornicing).

The building has five storeys and the rear mews has two storeys, with the upper ground mews floor corresponding to the ground floor of the main space. The original connection between the two was via an open courtyard, which SHH has now partly built over to form a covered walkway between the two for all-weather access.

Jamba Juice Support Centre

Project Name: Jamba Juice Support Center   **Designer:** Pollack Architecture
Location: Emeryville, CA, USA   **Photographer:** Cesar Rubio; Eric Laignel   **Time:** 2008
Area Size:3344 sqm

California-based Pollack Architecture was hired by Jamba Juice to transform a Class B office building of steel, glass, and veneer brick into an energetic office space that captures the brand's spirit while paying homage to the funky warehouse from which the national smoothie chain was moving. The architects renewed an existing building to reflect the dynamic culture of the company while creating an industrial/warehouse quality for the space. Signature shades of vibrant orange and lime green are featured throughout the office space, as are numerous graphics relating to the Jamba Juice brand. Doors throughout the space have been labeled with brand identifying names, such as Blender, Carrot, Banana, and Strawberry. The design connects the company's health-centric philosophy with key elements of its retail environment to create a fun and energizing workplace.

The spacious reception area features a signature "Jamba-green" wall that holds a branded image and welcomes visitors to both the office space as well as the brand. A near floor-to-ceiling steel industrial window wall system, typically used in warehouses, separates the reception from the conference and board rooms, while allowing natural light to penetrate throughout the spaces. Overhead, air ducts and structural beams remain exposed to immediately reveal warehouse characteristics for an industrial look.

The transition to the upper level includes a staircase, framed with a stainless-steel, glass, and wood guardrail, along a "Jamba-orange" wall. Individual workstations are located on this floor along with small-group meeting rooms.

Gummo Advertising Agency

Location: Amsterdam, Netherlands **Designer:** i29 interior architects **Photographer:** i29 interior architects **Completion date:** 2009

As Gummo were only going to be renting the space on the first floor of the old Parool newspaper building in Amsterdam for two years, i29 convinced Gummo to embrace the mantra of "reduce, reuse, recycle" to create a stylish office space that would impact as little as possible on the environment or their wallets. They developed a theme that reflects Gummo's personality and design philosophy — simple, uncomplicated, no-nonsense, yet unquestionably stylish with a twist of humour. Everything in the office conforms to the new house style of white and grey. All the furniture was locally sourced via Marktplaats (the Dutch eBay), charity shops and whatever was left over at the old office. Everything was then spray painted with polyurea Hotspray (an environmentally friendly paint) to conform with the new colour scheme. Even Jesus wasn't immune, as you can see in the attached pictures. The new office is a perfect case study of a smart way to fill a temporary space stylishly and at minimal cost. The collection of old and repaired products in its new coating has given a new potential and soul to the old furniture.

Larchmont Office

Project Name: Larchmont Office   **Designer:** Rios Clementi Hale Studios   **Location:** Los Angeles, CA, USA   **Area Size:** 17,000 sf

The architects transformed the building into a space of light by tearing down the exterior walls and installing a floor-to-ceiling window wall system, while maintaining the structure's existing footprint. The main entrance leads patrons to the receptionist counter. The white surfaces of the area allow light to travel deeper into the building through the front doors and around the space over lacquered finishes and bright colors. Next to the reception area is a large open conference room with 37-foot-high sliding glass doors. A fully-equipped kitchen is located around the corner to the west, featuring notNeutral products and designs. Around the corner to the east is a small powder room that showcases a floor-to-ceiling wall of green turf. Also located on this level is another informal meeting space, which the staff refer to as the "tree house" since the room features a floor-to-ceiling front window and overlooks a large tree. The space houses comfortable chaise loungers and a round wood table.

The upstairs offers two informal conference rooms surrounded by workstation pods. The goal was to create a nonhierarchical studio environment, so the architects designed two different pad scenarios where either six individuals are grouped together in the same area or the one large pod that incorporates 19 individual workstations.

Natural light is provided throughout the second floor with the surrounding glass-encased balconies, providing an indoor-outdoor atmosphere and offers additional gathering and break spaces. Light is also brought in by the existing and newly installed skylights. The exposed ducts and structural systems with the use of foil at the ceiling create an industrial feel to the space, bringing the firm's idea of the office space being its "idea factory" to life.

New Google Meeting Room

Project Name: New Google Meeting Room   **Designer:** Camenzind Evolution Ltd.
Location: Switzerland   **Photographer:** Camenzind Evolution Ltd.   **Time:** 2008

A key element in the design approach was that the Zooglers should participate in the design process to create their own local identity. Under the guidance of the Director of International Real Estate at Google in Mountain View, an interactive and transparent approach to the architectural process was implemented from the beginning. A diverse team of local Zooglers were formed as the steering committee to represent the entire office.

Zooglers needed to be diverse and at the same time harmonious whilst making it a fun and an enjoyable place to work in. The survey also showed that while personal workspace needed to be functional and more neutral, communal areas had to offer strong visual and more aesthetically enjoyable and entertaining qualities to stimulate creativity, innovation and collaboration.

The Zooglers decided early on that they preferred to reduce their personal net area of workspace in order to gain more communal and meeting areas. The working areas were therefore designed with a high degree of space efficiency. Additionally, they had to be able to accommodate frequent staff rotation and growth. On average a Googler moves twice a year within the building, consequently the office layout was designed for maximum adaptability so that all groups and departments can use any part of the office space. The office areas are organized along a central core and are a mixture of open-plan workspaces for 6-10 people and enclosed offices for 4-6 people.

Baroda Ventures

Project Name: Baroda Ventures   **Designer:** Rios Clementi Hale Studios   **Location:** Beverly Hills, CA, USA   **Time:** 2008   **Area Size:** 4,175 sf

The architects adapted a surprising, yet delightful, combination of retro and contemporary styles for the renovation of the two-storey Baroda Ventures office and applied several themes throughout the design — classic modern furnishings with unexpected fabrics, elaborate ceiling medallions and doors escutcheons, glossy surfaces, and repeated patterning at various scales — while incorporating plentiful daylight. Timeless elegance was achieved by pairing traditional essentials with the latest in design to create a place of sophisticated opulence.

A custom-designed steel-and-glass staircase provides access to the second floor, affording uninterrupted views of the fountain below. At the top of the staircase, through a wooden door adorned with an exaggerated escutcheon, is the reception area, featuring a two-seat Eames Sofa in striped upholstery and an aqua leather Barcelona Chair. The ceiling was removed and seismically restructured to expose the existing hip roof. New skylights were installed to bring views of the sky and daylight deeper into the office. Interior walls are clad with either white back-painted glass, limed oak panels, or modern versions of tongue-and-groove, which function as textural foils for the existing masonry shell.

The nine private offices, surrounding the reception area and extending to the back, have been individually characterized while encompassing design elements found throughout the space. The architects contrasted exposed brick in each office with lacquered finishes and the use of glass. Used at the top three feet of interior walls and at the center of doors, abundant glass keeps the space open and well lit. An interior light well becomes the internal circulation core as a skylight allows natural light to travel throughout the space, bouncing off the white-painted glass walls of the stairwell.

Office Herengracht 433, All Capital

Project Name: Office Herengracht 433, All Capital   **Designer:** i29 interior architects / eckhardt&leeuwenstein architects   **Location:** Amsterdam, the Netherlands   **Photographer:** i29 interior architects   **Time:** October 2008   **Area Size:** 240 sqm

The board of All Capital, an investment group in capital stock, wanted to have a self-called "power office". i29 interior architects and Eckhardt&Leeuwenstein, two offices which collaborated during this project, created this by placing every board member in the spotlight on a playful way.

All three boardrooms and a lounge are executed in an overall design concept. Large round lampshades, spray painted gold on the inside, seem to cast light and shadow oval marks throughout the whole space. By this, a playful pattern of golden ovals contrasts with the angular cabinets and desks, which are executed in black stained ash wood. In the flooring the oval shaped forms continue by using light and dark grey carpet. Also, these ovals define the separate working areas.

The lounge area has, in combination with the white marble flooring, these same light/shadow patterns that cover the bar and benches in silver fabrics. This area can be used for presentations or social working, with an integrated flat screen in the bar and data connections in all pieces of furniture. The existing space is set in a 17th century historic building, at one of the most famous canals of Amsterdam called "de gouden bocht". All existing ornaments and details are painted white.

The keynotes for this company are money and power. The design concept expresses this by setting all members of the board literally in the spotlights. The golden and silver ovals shatter through the spaces like golden coins. Where it is all about, in investment and stock trading.

Saatchi + Saatchi LA

Project Name: Saatchi + Saatchi LA   **Designer:** Shubin + Donaldson Architects
Location: Torrance, CA, USA   **Area Size:** 106,000 sf

Focusing great attention on the main floor — centrally located on the third level — the architects designed a communal hub to bring staff together on one floor in a variety of configurations. This main space allows for impromptu collaborative moments.

From either entrance, the company's theme of "homing at work" is apparent. A spiral library brings to life the concept of a hearth and acts as a central gathering space. The walls form spirals in both plan and elevation toward its center. This central vortex of energy is further emphasised as the cone-shaped form from the ceiling beams down a soft glow of light toward this center space, known by the staff as "the pit".

Other communal spaces offered on this floor include a living room-like lounge area that mixes classic and retro furnishings by Vitra, large full-service kitchen and dining area, gaming room with pool table and plasma television, multi-media room with a ceiling-mounted projection screen, bar highlighted by a backlit orange wall, and a bamboo garden "backyard". This unusual space is defined by slender bamboo poles strapped together with steel bracing and a border of river rocks within a steel trough. Planters with lush greenery, fountain sounds, picnic table, and smaller tables with pillow-like seating, provide a tranquil oasis to inspire creativity. All levels offer private and group work stations, fostering communication and deterring competition. The senior staff have semi-private offices behind floor-to-ceiling glass walls.

Office Lab

Project Name: Office Lab   **Designer:** architects lab   **Location:** Brussels, Belgium
Photographer: Tim Vandevelde   **Time:** 2008   **Area:** 190 sqm

Architects lab located their new office at the ground floor of the block situated between the two courtyards. The large windows and fixed glass parts not only allow large amounts of light to brighten the office space but also make the transition between garden and workspace to be much less abrupt. Since most designs created by architects lab can be described as puristic, free of clutter, hence also the studio's name, they made sure also their office was an example of this design philosophy.

The flooring, 10 by 10 cemented laboratory tiles in black, is the main feature. They are used not only for the floor but also certain wall parts are covered in these tiles. The largest wall in the office features a large library wall in dark wengé wood, over 4 metres high. It houses all technical and other information needed in the office. These two main features are joined by simple but efficient office furniture, mostly also from the designer's hand. The best example is the light fixture which hangs in the office meeting/lunchroom, a simple but elegant construction in white tubular steel and TL lightbulbs. Overall the look of the interior is contemporary but it does also really refer to the atmosphere which must have been found in 1920's labs and offices.

Turner Duckworth Offices

Project Name: Turner Duckworth Offices   **Designer:** Jensen Architects   **Location:** San Francisco,USA   **Time:** 2005

Program & Requirements:

A graphic design firm purchased this concrete warehouse building in the Jackson Square District of San Francisco. The previous tenant had completely filled the building with a maze of closed rooms and private offices. The client's goal for the project was to convert the interior to an open office plan and uncover the double-height light-filled shell hidden by the previous build-out. The new interior was to reinforce the brand image and work style of the design firm and their own graphic identity.

Ideas & Design Objectives:

Red Glass Volumes

Taking red from the firm's graphic identity and mixing it with glass as a building material offering transparency, the architects proposed coloured translucent window film as the key ingredient in the spatial mix. Juxtaposed against the otherwise white minimal interior, these red room-volumes punctuate the space and provide a degree of privacy and separation between functions without subdividing the dramatic double-height volume of the building.

Cantilevered Glass Table and Glass Floor

A long cantilevered glass table is the main protagonist of the space. Centrally located in the open office area, it provides a multipurpose meeting space for the staff. The glass table hovers over a glass floor so that light from the large skylight directly overhead makes its way all the way down to the basement below. With a single gesture, a programmatic need, a light requirement, and vertical circulation (a staircase runs under the table) are all combined into a three-storey sectional composition.

Simple Construction, Soft Luminous Space

The existing building had a strong spatial and material character and where possible, it was left exposed. Only the rough concrete floor was covered with a white cementitious topping. The subtly off-white colour selected for paint, laminate furniture, and flooring, combined with the layered natural and artificial lighting, gives the space warmth unanticipated in its minimal composition.

The Information Box

Project Name: The Information Box   **Designer:** neri & hu design and research office
Location: Shanghai,China   **Photographer:** neri & hu design and research office   **Time:** 2009

The information box was conceived as an apparatus to provide information for the apartments being sold in this prestigious development outside of Shanghai. The white oak clad wall of the box is also seen as a backdrop for the models and drawings displayed in the room. The wooden box has a series of doors, some of which slides out acting as divider for the space while other swings out with the inside showcasing pertinent information relevant to the different products being displayed outside. The conference rooms, offices, restrooms and back of house spaces are all located inside the box housing the team behind the project. The floors are clad in blue slate. Dark ceilings bring the calm atmosphere of space. White oak in the room and tender green in the corridor will stimulate people's vision and excite people. Regardless of all, the wooden box or the product itself is concerned, both played a very good background effects.

FOX Latin America Channel Base Offices

Project Name: FOX Latin America Channel Base Offices   **Designer:** Alberto Varas & Asociados, arquitectos Estudio Angélica Campi   **Location:** Buenos Aires, Argentina   **Photographer:** Sosa Pinilla   **Time:** 2008

The new building's demands were: to obtain natural light for working areas and distribute the complex net supply of informatic, telephonic, and satelite services, the air conditioning, and the energy required by the new functions. Taking each one into working areas, offices and meeting rooms of the different layout areas.

So the problem became into an interior perforation game to get the entrance of the natural light and generate a spaciality according to the creative labours of each versatile sector, which means, a spacial system differentiated and interconnected between them, where inserted both unique faces of the building able to connect with the urban space. In the background facade, it was generated a vertical four-floor height garden, which delivers views and light to each floor of the building. And the front facade to the street, consists in a double facade, one operable and the other steady/fixed which regulates the entrance of light and reflects the building's technological character.

Passing from the front into the building's background it's a theoretic promenade which leads to the public world of technology, the sophisticated LED light and the data projections over the façade into the calmness of the garden and the silence of the internal working areas where people can briefly and illusoriness escape from the guessing and seductive digital machine in which insides works.

China Everbright Limited (CEL)

Project Name: China Everbright Limited (CEL)   **Designer:** Lam Cham Yuen & Lee Ming Yan, Olivia
Location: Shenzhen,China   **Photographer:** Ulso Tsang Photographic   **Time:** 2007

Being located on the 46th floor of a main building Admiralty, one would expect stunning window-side scenery, and the YO Design team cleverly incorporated these striking views into the office design. A lot of transparent glass has been used throughout the interior and this helps to share the uplifting views brought in from the expansive windows. In addition to the reception, there are five main rooms and these include one big conference room, two smaller conference rooms, a middle working space, and a guest meeting room. Off from the reception, the main guest meeting room is the most informal area, with a striped carpet and spotlight-like lighting fixtures adding an element of fun to the interior. Like the facing reception lounge area outside, this room is symmetrically arranged, with the furnishings mirroring each other on either side of the room. Nearby, the main working area features the same lined carpet as the guest meeting room, and this helps to stretch the space of the room. There are interesting selections of accompanying light fixtures to boot.
The main conference room seats 40 and although there are no windows, this room is mainly used for video presentations and slide shows.

Ernst & Young University

Project Name: Ernst & Young University **Designer:** YO DESIGN LIMITED **Location:** SShanghai China **Photographer:** Ulso Tsang Photographi **Time:** 2007

As business challenges become more complex, the need for international firm to call upon the widest spectrum of views and opinions to address them is crucial. Employed over 135,000 talented people in 140 countries worldwide, sharing the same value for work and commitment to quality. The open culture offers continuous personal and professional development. As a global organization, "we support individuals who wish to apply their skills and experiences in new environments... Because when people grow and succeed, it is the company that benefits."

Due to the reason, this global organization wishes to provide spacious and warm learning environment for their employees through the use of natural materials such as wood and travertine cream. The space appears as if it is almost nestled within its surroundings. The atmosphere created has a tendency to let people relax from the uptight and occupied life style.

Motorized pivot doors are featured in oak wood veneer creating a warm and natural focus in the lounge area, while full length grey and clear mirror wall finishing amplified the depth of the space. Designer accented with red furnishing, bold lighting fixture and bright colour soft cushioned operable wall paneling creates a dynamic, yet truly joyful learning experience.

An International Firm— Shenzhen Branch

Project Name: An International Firm—Shenzhen Branch   **Designer:** Lam Cham Yuen & Lee Ming Yan, Olivia   **Location:** Shenzhen   **Photographer:** Ulso Tsang   **Time:** 2006

Located near reception is a pair of meeting/conference rooms, partitioned from the rest of the office with floor-to-ceiling glass panels. Besides allowing penetration of natural light, the glazing also has a psychological effect, symbolising the client's 'transparent' and 'open' way of doing business. Dark cushioned carpets bearing a pattern of white irregular lines adorn the floors, while a few walls are paneled in chestnut-coloured leather to add a balancing impression of gravity. Custom-designed charcoal stainless steel door frames and skirting elements add to the rooms' sharp definition to the rooms. For the sake of flexibility, the two conference rooms can easily be combined into a single multifunctional space by simply opening up the wall panels that usually divide them.

A narrow, lengthy passage decorated with uplights, grew reflective mirrors and veneer-look, plastic laminated wall panels links the general office area with three training rooms, which can be merged into a volume large enough to accommodate up to 100 people. At the core of the building – and easily accessible from the general office – is a roomy "time-out" area where employees can eat and relax. To make its special status clear, the area is located on a raised wooden platform.

Chengdu Sales Office

Project Name: Chengdu Sales Office   **Design Firm:** One Plus Partnership Limited
Location: Chengdu, China   **Photographer:** Mr. Law Ling Kit   **Time:** 2007   **Materials:** Black tiles, paint, stainless steel, gold colour mirror   **Area Size:** 467 sqm

All that can make an impact on the senses of a visitor as he crosses the threshold into a space is grist for the mill of instant assessment. Fairly or not, just as a cluttered and dusty living room will make guests think twice about a homeowner's standard of personal hygiene, a shabbily furnished office reception area will inevitably lead to doubts about a company's self-confidence and acumen.

Doubt of a rather more positive kind will likely entre the thoughts of visitors to this new office designed by One Plus Partnership, simply because it looks so little like an office. The spacious reception area glows with simple white surfaces and a subtle lighting scheme. A series of discontinuous curved partitions – some suspended in the air and some extending to the floor – divides the space into distinct-but-flowing zones, many of which are saturated with natural light courtesy of floor-to-ceiling windows. Details like artfully positioned black velvet sofas add a touch of softness to the scheme while preventing it from seeming too antiseptic.

Accordingly, the emphasis was on the architectural rather than the decorative, with Law and Lung endowing the space with a sharp-edged composition of simple forms executed in a palette of subtle-but-refined materials. An outstanding example of the designers' approach is seen in the discontinuous oval shape that circumscribes the office's central core. "The feature creates a smooth flow of presentation while at the same time adding to the impressive geometry of the area," Lung says. Its curve first emerges as part of the ceiling in the reception zone, drawing the visitor's eye deeper into the space where the feature transforms into a partition dividing a cashier's counter from the rest of the area. Finally, when it reaches the end of the volume, it rises to ceiling level to make way for a panoramic view through floor-to-ceiling windows.

Machiya Office

Project Name: Machiya Office   **Designer:** Hayakawa Hua Shi
Location: Niigata, Japan   **Photographer:** Koichi Torimura, Hirotaka Satoh   **Time:** 2007

The project "Machiya Office" was designed in Niigata (an old town in the north of Japan) in 2007. The total area of this project is 350.31 sqm (including 189.02 sqm floor area). The constructive structure of the office is steel frame; Machiya is a traditional townhouse along the street. The designers designed it as an office which is a base of widely spreaded business so it has the function of the face for that.

The shape of the site is narrow in frontage and long in depth. The designers proposed a two-storey auditorium with skylight that runs through the long axis of this tube-like building, which allows sunshine in and air out. That is called "walk through garden". Each room is divided up and down stair to face on "walk through garden". The auditorium and office are separated by a glass partition in a wooden frame and has a curved surface. The shape is formed by approximation for each room's area. To control the well, the glass is inclined. The bright and dynamic interior space creates an impressive corporate image for visitors, an important element of the project for the client. The facade references the black, stain painted wooden fences that make up the old town street.

City Year Headquarters for Idealism

Project Name: City Year Headquarters for Idealism   **Designer:** Elkus manfredi Architects
Location: Boston, Massachusetts   **Photographer:** Adrian Wilson   **Time:** 2007

City Year Headquarters for Idealism is the new permanent home base for the community service organization that inspired the creation of the federal AmeriCorps program. Elkus Manfredi Architects provided interior design services for this five-story, 55,000-square-foot signature space. The design tells the City Year story and supports the organization's brand, mission, and goals.

In 2004, Elkus Manfredi began working with City Year, real estate professionals, and the City of Boston to analyze building and development options. Once the appropriate building was identified, the team began to develop the concept for City Year's Headquarters for Idealism. To create a space with the same spirit and energy as City Year's young volunteers, a variety of graphics are incorporated into the design. Adorning everything from walls and glass partitions to floors and furnishings, inspirational messages and images fill the Headquarters with meaning and purpose.

The Lavine Civic Forum serves as a "theater of idealism," hosting corps-wide gatherings, guest speakers, and morning warm-ups. The room features large-scale video screens, moveable partitions and acoustic panels, whiteboards, a stage, and a pantry. Upper floors feature an open office plan that maximizes access to natural light. The second and the fifth floor are organized around collaborative spaces called "action pods".

The project is awaiting LEED-CI Silver certification.

PITW #52 Lead with ideas.

The first role of a leader is to lead with ideas, rather than rules or expectations. Allow people to get as excited as you are about those ideas. When people understand the "why" they will tend to quickly make the "how" happen.

"be the change you wish to see in the world."

MAHATMA GANDHI

Çağdaş Holding Office

Project Name: Çağdaş Holding Office   **Designer:** Nagehan Acimuz   **Location:** İstanbul, Turkey
Time: : 2006   **Area Size:** 420 sqm

Çağdaş Holding is active in many fields like construction, real estate, concrete, etc. The priority design criteria in the office area created with gross concrete walls, coexistence of wood and glass, natural stone floor and permeable wooden divider is transparency. Differentiating room dividers were made transparent and for aesthetic considerations and privacy, permeable divider panels were added to these transparencies .

Meinl Bank

Project Name: Meinl Bank   **Designer:** ISA STEIN Studio   **Location:** Linz, Austria
Photographer: ISA STEIN   **Time:** 2007   **Area Size:** 2000 sqm

To create a new business branch for a bank was a total new task for ISA STEIN Studio. Especially the bank is known for its exclusivity and tradition. What they tried to do was to bring these elements into a new design and they alao wanted that the innovation gets shown of course besides the traditional approach. Therefore they used a lot of detailed features like using their symbol of a blackamoor in surprising ways. Not only the client's zones are treated with elaborate materials, but also the recreation zones for the employees. Behind the big photo wall in the office space, you will find the kitchen and sitting area. So you have both sides for an approach. While working you are facing the image "buy low – sell high" and while being on a brake, you are seeing the image from behind.

The client zone is very flexible. The meeting rooms can be changed into one big meeting room, or left separate. The entrance area also has a nice place to sit into leather lounge chair, in order to create a more genuine atmosphere.

DITTEL – Architekten

Project Name: DITTEL – Architekten   **Designer:** d-arch   **Location:** Stuttgart, Germany   **Time:** 2008

In a former horse stable in the Western part of Stuttgart DITTEL – Architekten found its new home. The new and modern bureau forms a contrast to the old building and offers a beautiful view over Stuttgart. The classical loft with an area of 230 square metres was completely renovated. The structure of the building was reconstructed and provided with a clear and clean alignment.

Different working areas (reception, modelling space, lounge, conference area, working tables) are separated by shelves which offer either an open or closed structure due to a flexible system. This system consists of a frame and varying cubes in three different sizes. In this way the look can be changed and the interior always meets the requirements of the daily life of the architects as it can be adjusted according to their needs.

The CI colours of DITTEL – Architekten, grey, white and light green, are reflected in the bureau. All pieces of furniture are finished in high-gloss, accentuated by a lime colour used in the inside of the cubes. Both the screed floor which is sanded, polished, and glazed/sealed and the 150 year old oak conference table emphasise the character of the building.

DITTEL – Architekten created a bureau where everybody likes to work, feels comfortable and is perfectly representative for its clients.

Headquarters Expansion

Project Name: Headquarters Expansion   **Designer:** KlingStubbins   **Location:** Princeton, USA
Photographer: KlingStubbins   **Time:** 2008

The building will embody the principles of Danish design – functionality, innovation, openness, quality, and aesthetics; Nordic tradition – natural light, clear colors, integrity in choice of materials; and functional architecture – simple shapes, clean lines and logical solutions. The overall building is organized into three basic zones. The entrance and support zone on the first floor includes public functions such as reception and security, receiving, regulatory file rooms, and a café for the building. The second zone is the full floor training center located on the second floor. The third zone is the office area on floors three, four, and five.

For the office zone, a centrally located common area housing conference rooms, informal meeting areas, a pantry, mail room, and lunch space serves as the heart – Hjerte in Danish – of each floor. Each wing includes huddle rooms, project rooms, touch down spaces, and hoteling spaces. Wireless technology has been incorporated throughout the facility for data and telecommunications allowing staff, visitors, and contractors to work anywhere with full access to the Novo IT network.

The new Novo Nordisk headquarters draws on the best current workplace thinking and practice to create a sustainable and productive environment. Environmental stewardship is a core value for Novo Nordisk and the project has been submitted for LEED® Certification. Sustainable strategies include daylight harvesting, recycling of construction waste, use of sustainable materials, low VOC materials, regional materials, and green power.

The LG Air-conditioner Academy

Project Name: The LG Air-conditioner Academy   **Designer:** Illés Attila, Sotkó Anikó
Location: Budapest, Hungary   **Photographer:** Illés Attila , Juhász Tamás   **Time:** 2007

The building is situated on the Könyves Kálmán street, including training room, exhibition room, kitchen-dining room, toilet and bathroom, and reception.

Opposite the front glass door, a glass covered reception desk wellcomes the visitor. The reception desk is made of brick and mahagoni wood panel. Above the reception desk there is a special Artemide lamp, the desk from below is lighted with spot lamps built into the floor. In a niche behind the reception desk the emblem of LG can be seen, lighted with hidden spot lamps. On the right side of the reception in a glass cabinet the small products of LG can be found. The back wood panel of glass cabinet runs up to the ceiling where the spotlights are placed.

The kitchen-dining room is behind the reception area. separated by a medial wall with glass walls on both sides. Next to the reception (foyer) foreground there is an exhibition room. In the exhibition room around the wall and on the metal podium and on the ceiling there are LG products and air conditioners.

The material in the middle of the floor beech patterned laminated, around the walls the floor is gravelled patterned linoleum. The training room opens from exhibition/show room. The training room has space for up to 33 people. The floor and the desks are covered with beech patterned laminated wood. From the dining room striped sandglass door opens to the corridor of the water system. In the water system there are modern decor (wassbasin, toilet) and special surfaced and metallic impression ceramic panels.

The atmosfhere of the whole interior of the building is modern, functional, practical, clear, friendly, cosy and at the same time fashionable, grandiose.

Ding Pu Hi-tech Square

Project Name: Ding Pu Hi-tech Square   **Designer:** Lin Eddy E+ interior design studio
Location: Taiwan, China   **Photographer:** Liu Her-rang   **Time:** 2008

In Chinese geomantic culture, there are five basic elements. The five elements are of the relationships of generation and restriction. Basically, Wood generates Fire; Fire generates Earth; Earth generates Gold; Gold generates Water; Water generates Wood. Using the generation and restriction theory, these five elements can coexist peacefully and the magnetic field will be stable. The interior space is designed according to this theory. Wood is in green and embodied by Jade; Fire is in red and embodied by Coral; Earth is in yellow and embodied by Topaz; Gold is in White and embodied by Crystal; Water is in black/blue and embodied by Sapphire. The five large glass Acrylic artworks are hanging in the hall's ceiling, sitting the southeast. The five elements are used with their unique location, colour, shape, texture and sound. The artworks echo rich light in the modern glass hall.

The two columns show the boss's expectation to his staff: "flexible outwardly and strict inwardly". The reception is quite functional. Besides it is the negotiation zone, with digital video to broadcast real-time information. On the right is the floor designation wall. To show the image of Water, the wall is designed in carved 3D waves. Incorporating the interactive sensory sound system and the changing light of the glass wall, the space is added by more sensual joy. The wall of the left negotiation zone with image of Wood is carved into a bamboo forest. The forest is dense and vibrant with birds' and insects' song. The negotiators will feel pleasant and comfortable.

TIC

Project Name: TIC   **Designer:** Noriyuki Otsuka Design Office Inc   **Location:** Tokyo, Japan
Photographer: Noriyuki Otsuka   **Time:** 2009

Facing Nihonbashi Entrance Square of Tokyo Station, this centre is close to the shopping area crowded with long-established department stores and works as a hub for the access to the central Tokyo including Nihonbashi, Ginza, and Marunouchi business district as well as to the local areas throughout Japan conveniently. As the centre of tourist information in which visitors collect the new data with fun, it aims to enhance the internal/foreign tourism and to widen the tourist sites around Japan and the world starting from Tokyo.

The space was designed to make Tokyo's portal cool. The designer tried not to use traditional Japanese motif, like Zen space. The ceiling and the wall are painted in white; the flooring is in a special made gold plastic tiles. In red painted receptionist space, a counter made with white glass is placed with receptionists who speaks skillful in 4 languages (Japanese, English, Chinese and Korean), to allow them a detailed service. In the centre of the lobby, few laptop computer are placed on a round counter, visitors can access freely on TIC TOKYO Official Site with them. Under Japanese map, the self-service brochure rack is full of company and autonomy's brochure from all over the Japan.

The high ceiling who gives a kind of tension is decorated with photography of sponsors. Visitors seem to find contemporary designed TIC TOKYO Japanese. White color seems to mention Japanese castles, red color booth, Japanese flags. Well, Gold floor would mean `Chipangu (gold country)`told in `Description of the world` of the famous explorer, Marco Polo.

Shiyuan restaurant

Project Name: Shiyuan restaurant   **Designer:** Lispace design studio,LiJia   **Location:** Beijing, China
Photographer: HanGao   **Time:** 2008

Shiyuan Restaurant, located in the urban and rural trade centre of Beijing and famous for Sichuan cuisine, has a great number of regular customers. With the rapid development of its surrounding region, the owner decided to completely renovate the interior with the requirement of combining local elements of Sichuan. Finally, the designer proposed the theme of "Extraordinary Mountains and Rivers in Sichuan".

 With 520 square metres in total, the restaurant is composed of two parts: formal dinning room and fast food area. The designers broke the original closed layout with a full tempering glass wall in place of the concrete wall separating the restaurant and the department store beside. Moreover, part of the space is complete free of any kind of partitions to make it more spacious and transparent.

In the formal dinning room, the design shows great concerns in maintaining the privacy of the customers. From this point, the designers employed different dividing structures, for example, the aluminum sheets dangling from the ceiling. In addition, the floor and the ceiling are respectively covered with black Vitrified tile and white plaster in order to highlight other decorative elements. The multifunctional dinning area is specially designed for different events.

The fast food area, however, addresses fluidity, high speed and communication. The designers imaginatively play with "a piece of paper" (space) and fold it into different "parts". The counter, the desk and the ceiling are all covered with white artificial stones.

Maedaya Bar

Project Name: Maedaya Bar   **Designer:** Architects EAT   **Location:** Victoria, Australia
Photographer: Derek Swalwell   **Time:** 2008   **AreaSize:** 120 sqm

This project demonstrates the possibility of using ordinary recyclable material for hospitality projects without compromising the sophistication of the food and service.

Traditionally sake is bottled in wooden casks and secured with ropes. Current commercial method of bottling sake is similar to that of red or white wine. Designers' interest in sake bottling lies in the bounding of the cask using ropes. Thereafter they chose to investigate and translate their interpretation of 'bounding' with the use of Manila ropes. The ropes held in tension at specific points form a shape of a house or a hut. A house, whether it be a tea house or sake house is a sacred place in traditional Japanese times. It is a place where people drank in harmony.

The first floor function room is a space for self service grill. The essence of the space is in starck contrast with the ground floor. Here designers wanted to achieve a sense of humbleness: white washed walls, Japanese black stained timber flooring, simple timber benches and raw stainless steel canopies. There is no attempt to apply any embellishments because designers wanted the cooking to embody the purpose of this space.

Adour Alain Ducasse

Project Name: Adour Alain Ducasse   **Designer:** Rockwell group
Location: California US   **Photographer:** Bruce Buck ,Eric Laignel   **Time:** 2008

The main dining area is surrounded by wine displays in temperature-controlled armoires. Given the existing turn-of-the-century architecture of the St. Regis, special care was taken to create an environment that is both contemporary and dynamic, and sensitive to the building's architectural and historic context.

Elegant vitrine portals have been inserted into the existing stone wall entry and corridor to open the space up to Astor Court. In the main dining room, the existing architecture is covered in silver leaf and the walls are sheathed with a backlit, seeded glass veil etched with an abstract grapevine pattern, allowing one to look through the new to the old. Leather-covered furnishings in wine tones help create a warm, glowing atmosphere.

The main dining area has three private dining rooms. Two oval-shaped rooms with mirrored ceilings and fabric-covered walls are located in the corners of the back of the dining room. The oval rooms will be visually connected by a five-panel mural by the acclaimed New York artist Nancy Lorenz.

A third rectangular dining room features 50 leather and bronze wine lockers that enable guests to store either 12 regular bottles or 6 magnums of wine, as well as personal wine accessories, and a custom-designed album to record and preserve wine labels.

Adour at The St. Regis Washington, D.C.

Project Name: Adour at The St. Regis Washington, D.C.   **Designer:** rockwell group
Location: Washington   **Photographer:** Bruce Buck   **Time:** 2008

The designer preserved the original wood paneling and the base of the bar while updating the 84 square metres space with modern touches of stone and matte black lacquer, subtle metallic wall finishes, and furniture upholstered in sumptuous violet hues. The bar area is strewn with violet, grey, black and cream materials and finishes, in contrast to the 153 square metres main dining room, which is dominated by shades of white, black, and silver. The main dining room is designed with the same sensitivity to its historic heritage. Designer preserved the beautiful ceiling-height arched windows lining one wall letting in an abundance of natural light, the original woodwork throughout the space, and the existing 16 foot-high beamed ceiling, which also continues into The Bar. The landmark ceiling is composed of carved wooden flowers and decorations, providing an elegant classical contrast to the modern design elements that designer added, such as the 20-foot long Chesterfield-style dining banquettes along one wall upholstered in opalescent white leather and illuminated by rock crystal lamps. Other new additions to the space include three curved wood-wrapped dining niches that contain sleek black, channel-tufted banquettes and metallic wall coverings. Wenge and imbuye wood architectural details are juxtaposed against the matte black lacquer added to the existing woodwork in the space.

Dos Caminos

Project Name: Dos Caminos **Designer:** Rockwell group **Location:** Las Vegas, US
Photographer: Eric Laignel **Time:** 2008

The entrance to the restaurant is an arch of backlit glass tile framing an aqua bottle waterfall, which leads one to and lines the long restaurant entry walkway that elevates the patron from the casino floor. On the left, the aqua bottle waterfall is set against intense red textured plaster, while on the right it is open to the snake lounge beyond. Once you pass through the hand hammered iron gates with custom cast snake handles at the top of the ramp, you enter into the lounge, which is an intimate room with a backdrop of wide metal cerused wood plank walls. Weaving through the lounge are long curved banquettes with snake skin leather and upholstered mohair pillows.

The main dining room is designed to be a fantasy market. The walls and ceiling are covered with panels taken from the markets of Mexico including street art and found objects with imagery of classic Mexican cinema, wrestling and food. Accentuating the main dining room ceiling is a serpentine chandelier with glowing glass gems which leads the way down to the back dining room, reminiscent of Aztec temples.

The rear dining room is a celebration of eternal light with endless candles, the light of which is reflected between the walls and off of copper coloured glass.

Matsuhisa

Project Name: Matsuhisa   **Designer:** rockwell group   **Location:** Mykonos. Greece
Photographer: Vagelis Paterakis   **Time:** 2007

The designers converted the restaurant which was only a sushi counter into a full restaurant, incorporating the clients' specialised menu and iconic accents in the interior, furniture, and décor. The space includes a main interior space, one garden area with five bougainvillea vines growing over it, and two terraces, all used for dining.
To reach the main dining room and terraces, guests enter through the garden, which includes a new white marble sushi counter. Throughout each area, the designers have renovated the seating. They also designed hand crafted matchbook screens that Silverhill fabricated which wrap the entire interior space and create the ceiling and walls. Silverhill also painted images of cherry blossom trees on panels below the screens. In front of the matchstick screens are light fixtures made by Bocci (Italy), which are cast glass balls with halogen lights housed in cylindrical voids in the middle.
The back terrace is a classic lounge/bar with low seating, small scorched ash tables, and another marble bar. The second terrace is another outdoor dining area. Both terraces have beautiful vistas looking downhill over the town of Mykonos.

–ALL·DAY–
~STARTERS~

∘ Kicked·Up· ∘
Caesar

Honey Cornbread
Croutons,
Creamy Chipotle Dressing

∘ Jailhouse Red Chili ∘

Smoked
Brisket,
Pinto Beans

Chicken Wings
–Rubbed & Fried–
OR
–Slathered–
with
·Chipotle·Raspberry·

Frank's Redhot

∘ Bottle Caps ∘

Beer–Battered
fried
Jalapeño Slices,
Ranch Dressing

∘ The Hutto TexasWedge ∘

Iceberg,
candied Pecans, Bacon,
Blue cheese Dressing

Wildwood Barbeque

Project Name: Wildwood Barbeque **Designer:** rockwell group **Location:** Sao Paulo, Brazil
Photographer: Eric Laignel **Time:** 2008

Rockwell group show us a new BBQ by their new concept, which leads us to a new kind of BBQ in the city. The inspiration opens a new door for traditional concept. Wildwood BBQ is a 325 square metres space which is an intersection of both the rustic and the industrial. While the rustic theme is underscored by the restaurant's expansive wood-timber ceiling, the industrial aesthetic is emphasised by the use of steel-frame garage doors filled with nicotine-stained glass panes above the 50-foot bar and the original concrete floor. Blackened steel details, found on much of the furniture and architectural elements, serve to further illustrate the industrial theme.

 At Wildwood BBQ, designers embraced the challenge of re-purposing ordinary and found materials in creative ways. The restaurant also implements several raw and environmentally-conscious materials, such as plywood-clad walls, reclaimed wood, and even a bar top made of 100% recycled paper. What results is the birth of a new kind of BBQ environment; one that is influenced by it's urban setting. This is how we do barbeque in the city.

Tiandi Yijia – Restaurant

Project Name: Tiandi Yijia – Restaurant **Designer:** Mauro Lipparini **Location:** Shanghai China
Photographer: Gionata Xerra **Time:** 2007

Light and shadow define the mood of a space while silently interpenetrating one another in order to engage the occupant of the space. The magical key to the Tiandi Bund n° 6 project is "luxury". The use of contemporary light fixtures and indirect light sources increase the interplay of light and shadow: light is projected though cuts and slits in the false ceiling patterns, and filtered through crystal and glass.

The "set design" of the restaurant is developed as follows: on the left-hand side you will find a large wall clad with natural travertine stone; on the right-hand side you will find a lounge-type area that has the warm, comfortable feeling of a living room outfitted with sofas. In the central area behind the staircase, you can catch a glimpse of the clear, luminous foyer articulated by crystalline lighting all of which create a jewel-like feminine environment. The foyer has a gazebo-like design with a vaulted ceiling made up of light-green glass pilasters and glass panels on three sides. The fourth side is composed of a sculpted travertine stone wall. From the foyer, one enters the Grand Hall, divided fundamentally into three naves: the central area expresses a magical and mysterious use of light. Both sides of the Grand Hall contain two long "niches" composed of pleated fabric and indirect lighting placed above the false ceiling, thus creating a whole new "adventure" of light — curling shadows, softly lit rippled dunes in the desert.

BEI — Asian Restaurant

Project Name: BEI — Asian Restaurant   **Designer:** Lyndon Neri and Rossana Hu
Location: Beijing, China   **Photographer:** Derryck Menere and Michael Webber   **Time:** 2008

Walking into Bei, one is surrounded by a forest of trees — wooden members physically and visually screening those within from the outside. Passing through the second screen one enters a clearing, the Public Dining area above which bird lights dance, seemingly caged within the screen. Facing the Raw Bar a large mirror behind the chefs allows the patrons to celebrate the art of the cuisine.

Visible beyond the clearing are five white boxes, carved within to house the private dining rooms. Windows above lead one's eye to urban scenes, and small openings in reflective compositions on the wall allow the diners to view into the other's space.

Sureno (Mediterranean Restaurant)

Project Name: Sureno (Mediterranean Restaurant)   **Designer:** Lyndon Neri and Rossana Hu
Location: Beijing,China   **Photographer:** Derryck Menere and Michael Webber   **Time:** 2008

Concrete walls define the more public, circulatory areas of Sureño while the spaces beyond with their surfaces of warm woods and blue olive grove patterns remind one of the Mediterranean. Winding through the entry, the hearth of the restaurant is revealed – the Pizza Oven – with its surrounding counter, allowing patrons to gather and watch the chefs at work. Breaks in the ceiling allow light to stream through and the ceiling's slope upward in the public dining area emphasises the view of the Sunken Garden. The wooden floor extends into the Sunken Garden to become a deck and the water pools within the restaurant and outside at the Sunken Garden ensure their connection to each other and the Sea is not missed.

Cityscape Restaurant

Project Name: Cityscape Restaurant   **Designer:** Matt Gibson Architecture+Design Studio
Location: Melbourne, Austrilia   **Photographer:** John Wheatley   **Time:** 2008

The design intent was to maximise the configuration of the existing restaurant space to provide for an effective educational layout whilst also making best use of the existing facilities which included views to, from and within the restaurant.

The existing restaurant (unrenovated since the early 80's) was located behind closed doors and had been accessed via a long dark corridor leading adjacently into the existing space. Once inside, the existing restaurant did however contain stunning panoramic views of the City of Melbourne skyline. These contextual elements informed the decisions to first, open up the restaurant space to the rest of the building internally via the use of a large glazed entry and display area , and second, to reposition the existing bar so that it orientated itself and the entire restaurant configuration toward the view of the city. Devices such as an angled mirror above the bar-top is used for student lessons to gain a 'birdseye' view of the bar top action, but it also reflects the view of the city from the bar meaning the city is in view from all directions.

Existing rooms within the restaurant are retained where possible and simply re-cycled for other functions. The existing operable wall spanning across the restaurant was retained and re-clad, and another operable wall was added to enable the flexibility to break up the space into 3 separate isolated workshop areas. With this wall closed the Private Dining & Meeting room is used for small conferences with a pull down projection screen, or it can provide an elegant makeshift 'Boardroom' for administrative or lunch meetings with external business entities. Alternatively, the restaurant space can be extended by 12 covers when the operable wall is open.

NEVY

Project Name: NEVY   **Designer:** Concrete Architectural Associates
Location: Amsterdam the Netherlands   **Photographer:** Ewout Huibers   **Time:** 2008

Concrete was asked to redesign the formerly known restaurant Onassis. The restaurant is a new member in the succession of two existing restaurants; delicacy restaurant "envy" and wine bar "vyne". The facility for this location is a fish restaurant called "nevy".

Concrete created tranquillity by eliminating all unnecessary elements. The basic of the design concept is to create a space, which has the appearance of an old market hall. Marble was therefore a forehand choice.

The restaurant exists of two parts, the restaurant and the raw bar. To create a visual separation between the two parts black and white are chosen. In the white part, the ceiling and floor are black. The opposite appears in the black area. There you see a white floor and ceiling.

In this part of the white restaurant, you can find the best view of the "Ij" and Amsterdam north. Concrete chose to place six couches, white marble tables and white high gloss revolt chairs cross-grained the façade. In this way guests can optimally enjoy the view.

The couches have a "deeper" seating so that the customers can relax longer after finishing dinner.

In the back of the restaurant you can find the raw bar. In this area the chef is the main focus point.

The raw bar experience is different compared to the white restaurant; the walls are made of black marble, the floor of white marble and the ceiling is painted white.

Vengeplus Capacity

Project Name: Vengeplus Capacity **Designer:** Nagehan Acimuz **Location:** İstanbul, Turkey
Photographer: Nagehan Acimuz **Time:** 2007

The designers created 330 sqm indoor and 440 sqm outdoor seating area which accomodates 400 customers in total. In the whole restaurant area the designers have used stone wall coverings seperated by wooden semi-transparent seperations which were designed to both seperate different types of seating units and get a wide point of view. Floors and 13 metre bar were covered by natural stone. The lay-out plan was formed by using free tables along entrance axis, a long social table, different sizes and shapes of small tables which could be combined and seperated according to the number of customer groups.

The deisgners place most of the small tables in front of the long banquette seatings. Some compartment like private seating areas were formed between wooden seperations. Ceilings covered by wooden pannels around the area were lowered on top of the built-in seating to create a sense of coziness. Some suspended lighting fixtures were chosen to have a dim light for late night dinners. The other parts of the ceilings, on the contrary, were kept high and light-coloured to help keep the spacious feeling. Wooden seperations and wall coverings were supported by sketch images of vegetables to add a sense of humour to the whole place.

SEVVA Restaurant

Project Name: SEVVA Restaurant   **Designer:** TsAO & McKOWN Architects   **Location:** Hong Kong, China   **Time:** 2008

A bare rooftop with superb views is transformed into multiple dining environments, each with a distinct menu and character. SEVVA was envisioned as a miniature city within a city, a composition of distinct "neighbourhoods". Each one embodies the essence of one of SEVVA's menus, thereby offering guests a panoply of experiences to choose from, much as any great city does.

Bank Side caters to Hong Kong's business and power elite, with vistas of Norman Foster's groundbreaking HSBC (Hong Kong Shanghai Banking Corporation) headquarters and the commercial district as backdrop.

Harbour Side offers a more casual dining experience; warm tones of ivory, ebony, and buttercup yellow serve as counterpoint to Bank Side's clean-lined Minimalism. A unique vaulted ceiling casts a soft, luminous glow over the room. Taste Bar transforms itself from a bento box bar at lunch time into an urbane cocktail lounge in the evening. A bold tropical palette, complete with faux rhinoceros horns and a lush vertical garden of aromatic maiden hair ferns from Belgium bring a whimsical touch of the exotic to this ultra-metropolitan setting. Cake Corner is a child's dream made real. Confections morph into décor in this delirious chamber of glass-encased treats. Surrounding it all is a wrap-around terrace: surrounded by iconic skyscrapers, harbour, and mountains close enough to touch, one feels viscerally connected with the entire metropolis at once.

BRAND STEAKHOUSE

Project Name: BRAND Steakhouse   **Designer:** GRAFT   **Location:** Las Vegas, Nevada   **Time:** 2008
Size: 7,500 sf

The BRAND Steakhouse sits amidst the casino floor in the Monte Carlo Hotel in Las Vegas. The marriage of texture and form coupled with numerous height variations affords a constantly diversified spatial experience. The perception is individualized and ever-changing due to the magnetic patterning of the ceiling panels as well as the rich and ambient materials, invoking the sensation of being present within a diversified ecology. The choice of materials — smoked oak flooring, leather, suede upholstery, tree branched mirror and LED animated panels, cow hide patterns — gives the space an essence of nature serving as a counterpoint to the hyper-synthetic casino environment.

The façade's low walls, whose distribution coheres to the ceiling panels above, resurrect the image of the wooden fence typical of a ranch. A low wall opens up to the casino and provides smooth transition into an enticing space.

The ceiling canopy could be termed as the jewel of the space. Consisting of numerous panels wrapped in custom-printed fur, the canopy reveals itself as an intricately distributed cowhide pattern, which is abstracted through the technique of pixilation. Panels lit at various depths create a spectacular dusting glow, intended to captivate the viewers and simultaneously evoke feelings of comfort, repose and visual movement. The panels gradually rise towards the back of the restaurant, unfolding the guests to the maximized view of the animated ceiling.

Inamo

Project Name: Inamo   **Designer:** Blacksheep   **Location:** London   **Photographer:** Francesca Yorke
Time: 2008

Inamo is 310 sq m (gross), 62-cover Wardour Street restaurant and downstairs bar, offering customers high-quality Asian fusion cuisine. It also offers a whole new paradigm in the way people can order food, with menus projected onto tabletops, allowing diners to order food and beverages interactively, to change the ambiance of their individual table, to play games or even to order up local information and services, such as booking a cab.

It was an ambitious project and a tricky concept to get right. Great attention had to be paid especially to ensure that lighting levels and proportions were spot on for the restaurant to work at all hours of the day and night. The restaurant design also had to have an overall strong sense of identity as a space, neither overwhelming nor being overwhelmed by the technology at its heart.

'Cocoon' projectors are set at the same height throughout within the suspended high gloss black ceiling and come in three sizes to light 2-cover, 4-cover or 6-cover tables. When customers sit down there are white spots for plates and an individual 'e-cloth' for each table. Customers use a touch panel to order food and drink or change their table top to one of the seven other patterns available.

The restaurant has been treated partly in monochrome to allow the tabletop illuminations to stand out and partly with further graphics (inspired by the colour choices of kaleidoscopes and origami for an Asian feel) to mirror the strong graphic sense created by the tabletops. Walls are therefore in a white vinyl wallpaper with mirrored graphic panels, which work effectively like lightboxes with an etched pattern and a cut pattern, with light allowing the cut pattern to shine through. Seats are either a silver vinyl banquette with feature red stitching or else 2-tone flip chairs with black backs and white frontage. The tables themselves have a black base and a white Corian top.

"pearls & caviar"

Project Name: "pearls & caviar" **Designer:** concrete **Location:** Arab **Photographer:** concrete
Time: 2008

"pearls & caviar" represents the new Arabian lifestyle, a luxury fusion of east and west, black and white, occident and orient, light and shadow, the extrovert and the introvert, the intimacy and the view.

The basic idea of the design of the restaurant was to create an abstraction of the commonly used oriental forms and materials without loosing their richness. To achieve this, the amount and the richness of the oriental patterns and forms which are found in traditional oriental spaces are kept but without color. All colours are replaced by either shades of black or shades of white — both in combination with silver. Therefore the restaurant is divided in two parts, which also gives it's its name: "pearls & caviar".

Lido

Project Name: Lido   **Designer:** JP Concept Pte Ltd   **Location:** Singapore
Photographer: JP Concept Pte Ltd   **Time:** 2007

Nestled in the tropical greenery of the Sentosa Golf Club, a sense of grandeur and luxury permeates this restaurant. The colour concept juxtaposes an off white colour scheme against a black background to create spatial depth and visually arresting contrast. Selected furniture are used to infuse a dash of contemporary vibe to the lavish setting. In the dining area, brown tinted mirrors on dark blackish colour timber veneer serve to provide a "scattering effect" to reflect the outdoor greenery into the room. A long suspended tinted glass top counter provides storage solutions while maintaining the elegance of the setting.
Parallel to the walls are long black suede modular booth seats forming a passage between dining area and the bar. Placed opposite these long booth seats are specially selected transparent polycarbonate "Louis Ghost" chairs. The modish chairs make a perfect "transitional" element bridging and balancing the more ornate design aspects with the chic.
On the white table settings in the middle of the room is the alternating orange & green "Mademoiselle" armchairs. Crowned with richly coloured upholstered top, rectangular backrests and concave sides on transparent legs, these armchairs complete the smooth blend of classy styles with a burst of contemporary chic.
The lounge on the other side is an intermingling of both bright and dark elements. The main focus is the bar counter inspired by the human curvature. The counter's customised fibreglass moulding is illuminated by built-in lighting. 5 sleek black and 1 white "Spoon" high stools add elegance to the meandering centre piece. The ZEPPELIN chandelier, is used as the central lighting in the lounge. Unlike traditional sharp edged and elaborately wired chandeliers, the cocooned chandelier presents a softer natural feel.

VLET Restaurant

Project Name: VLET Restaurant   **Designer:** JOI-Design GmbH, Hamburg   **Location:** Hamburg, Germany   **Photographer:** JOI- Design GmbH   **Time:** October 2008   **Area:** 390 sqm

In Old High German the word "Vlet" meant a fleet, or a channel in coastal cities. One manner of introducing the context of the restaurant's name into the interior design is through the gigantic golden fish sculpture that greets guests at the entry. The space plan also capitalizes on the "stream-like" ripples created by the curves in the barrel-vaulted ceiling to create a directional flow though the dining area. Additionally, a floor lamp constructed from soft fabric to resemble a floating sea urchin is placed alongside the timber dining table by the feature window. The predominantly natural tones of the restaurant's décor allow the vibrant culinary creations to be the true artistic masterpieces. Reminiscent of the richness of the traders' treasures of coffee, carpets, spices and silks stored in these former warehouses, JOI-Design has created a canvas that allows the menu to shine.

The graceful arches of the barrel-vaulted ceiling, steel beam supports and textured brick and plaster walls are enhanced by newer design elements such as the rustic timber plank floors, rich leather chairs and driftwood "sculptures" lit from below to define their shadows against the irregular wall surface. The heavy, rough-hewn natural finishes of these structural design features are offset by the smooth, shiny modern materials of the stainless steel dining table bases and barstool frames, clear crystal wine glasses and sparkling translucent pendant lights. The visually exciting contrast is further emphasised by the bold flash of fresh lime green behind the bar and on its counter surface.

Chocolate Soup Café

Project Name: Chocolate Soup Café   **Designer:** pericles liatsos designers
Location: Limassol, Cyprus   **Photographer:** pericles liatsos designers   **Time:** 2008

Chocolate soup is a new concept cafe located in the centre of Limassol, Cyprus. The space is divided into 3 parts. The large sofa on one end, the central area with various shapes of sofas, poufs and chairs and the high tables area. The way the furniture was placed indicates a playful mood and atmosphere that makes the customer feel relaxed. The colours are simple and vibrant, with the various shaped sofas and the oversized chandelier giving it a more surreal feeling to a quite small space. Though not the standard cafe layout with large sofas and poufs combined with high tables and stools, classic armchairs and chandeliers, the visitor surely enjoys this strange composition.

The exterior canopy is see-through and of fuchsia colour which gives the whole space, exterior and interior, a different feeling depending what time of the day it is. It is decorative as well as functional. The canopy gives color to the white rattan sofas and armchairs at midday and protects from rain or humidity at night.

The space attracts customers for coffee and breakfast in the mornings, business lunches, afternoon coffees and on a smaller scale dinner and drinks. A very enjoyable and happy space, a tribute to chocolate!

Mc Donalds Urban Living Prototype

Project Name: Mc Donalds Urban Living Prototype   **Designer:** Studio Gaia, Inc
Location: New York, USA   **Photographer:**   **Time:** 2008

Studio GAIA was commissioned by the multi-billion corporation that helped shape American culture as well as the international food marketing in designing their brand new wardrobes that is not restricted by the industry standards but to create a brand experience that reflects fresh, modern and warm interior elements. The design focuses and celebrates on the freshness of the ingredients and promotes a fresh and healthy outlook to the household brand name. Upon entering, guests are greeted with a full height custom transparent divider panels with oversized produce graphics. Red wall tiling, light and wooden tile flooring as well as vibrant colors seating help create an open but warm dining and café experience.
The main inspirations behind Urban Living design are: Inviting, Lounging, Intimate and Relaxation. There are various main design features within the Urban Living design:
a. The yellow horizontal continues "band" that wraps the interiors from ceiling to the vertical high table (TV) wall then transitioning to the floor;
b. Light wood ceiling panels with oversized pendants above "lounging banquets" creating a warm and inviting feel;
c. Custom black and white graphic wall covering and semi-see thru panels creates privacy and graphic ideas based on store localization.

Oth Sombath Restaurant

Project Name: Oth Sombath Restaurant   **Designer:** Jouin Manku   **Location:** Paris, France
Photographer: Eric Laignel   **Time:** 2008

Searching for the right balance in ambience for the restaurant — it should at once respond to the restaurant's cuisine and offer something exquisitely modern. The designer immersed themselves in the universe of Thailand and translated it into the Parisian context. They studied the traditions and culture for colours, rhythms, volumes, light, while simultaneously looking to create a fully contemporary gastronomic experience. The interior decoration uses stunning elements, such as smooth lines and sleek curves, something sensual and exotic, something that feels like the delicate blend of all these rich influences embodied in one place.

The inspiration runs through the bar and three dining rooms, each offering a unique atmosphere to enjoy Oth's sumptuous flavours — one in scintillating gold, one in bold orange, and one in soft creams — the colour palette calling to mind in turn the temple treasures, bold colours of the women's dresses and rice paddies. Saffron-hued upholstered walls pop in the restaurant's multilevel interior. Textures also play reference in the restaurant – that of the curving wall of the bar looks like the hairstyles on Buddha sculptures while the warm wooden floor on the rez-de-chaussée echoes the dark wooden artisans' creations in Thailand. The arch of a dragon's back resonates with the sweeping curves of the stairway connecting the three dining rooms.

Restaurant Alain Ducasse

Project Name: Restaurant Alain Ducasse   **Designer:** : Patrick Jouin   **Location:** Dorchester UK
Photographer: Eric Laignel   **Time:** 2007

Concept

The restaurant at the Dorchester is a presentation of English culture as digested by the French. The project takes inspiration from the ever-present power of English gardens, parks as well as horse races, horse riding, picnics, classic cars, the country house, and a sprinkling of Midsummer's Night Dream. The aim of the project is to find a way to create a luxurious experience that takes clients out of the city and into a new imaginative locale – a place they may recognize from books or pictures they've seen, but at the same time is something they've never really seen before. Here they seek to create a luxurious experience from seemingly ordinary materials, crafting luxury not from gold and crystal but from the particular way they combine ordinary and sometimes coarse materials, the way they curve and converge, the way the colours blend into each other and the light brings in a soft accent. Luxury emerges as more about how things are put together – a particular situation created for this meal – rather than what is put together. They can give rise to luxury, to comfort, to lavishness, simply by creating an exquisitely-considered situation.

Spaces

The entrance to the restaurant is framed by greeter's desk and menu board which give way to a small corridor. The entry corridor is dim, but it is flanked by large oval windows that give partial glimpses into the room beyond, filtered by hovering screens of shimmering green dots which in turn allow a look into the park beyond. At the end of the corridor lies a large suspended curved disk. This screen of sorts bends gently in both directions and is wrapped in leather with intricate stitching details and an inlaid luminosity. A quiet whisper, a small phrase to gently welcome the guests to the restaurant as well as separate them from the rest of their day, evening, night...

The main dining room is filled with light. The walls are clad in seemingly traditional raw oak woodwork with a floor of wide oak planks. The ceiling caps the room in plaster. To one end of the room lies a series of bent screens.

Leggenda Ice Cream and Yogurt

Project Name: Leggenda Ice Cream and Yogurt   **Designer:** SO Architecture
Location: Ramat Ishay Israel   **Photographer:** Asaf • Oren   **Time:** 2009

In the industrial zone of Ramat Ishay northern Israel, inside an old abandoned carpentry shop a new branch of the Leggenda ice cream and yogurt was put up. It wasn't easy to design a space with an airy and calm feeling, as the customer desired, in the space the deisgners had to work with. This difficulty was caused by very low ceiling of only 2.30m, the very long and narrow proportion of 4.50m X 18.50m of the place. Another major difficulty was caused by the foundations of the building above the shop, which invaded into the inner space.

The main idea of the design was to create two linear elements that will lead the client into the deepest parts of the shop where the cozy sitting places are located. The large scale window in the entrance and on the side of the hall was opened to allow daylight in. The entrance is emphasised by its geometry. The large door and facade were slightly submerged into the inner space in order to entice the visitor into the place. The steel door and welcome roof were created as a single piece. The graphic wall behind the goods displays was designed by FIRMA, and adds fun to the atmosphere of the shop.

Rosso Restaurant

Project Name: Rosso Restaurant   **Designer:** So Architecture   **Location:** Ramat Israel
Photographer: Asaf Oren   **Time:** 2007

The Rosso restaurant is situated in Ramat Yishay, a town in the valley of Yezre-el in the Northern part of Israel.

The green hill around the place influenced the design. The planning seeks to explore – How to give to the restaurant space the feeling of its surrounding. The design checks in what manner could it produce an atmosphere, or feeling, of being outside while sitting inside.

The atmosphere in the restaurant is pleasant. The furrowed fields, which are framed by the strip of windows, find its continuation in the ceiling, and embrace the diner as if by the foliage of trees, with the furrows flowing to the horizon.

The walls are covered in softly textured upholstery – dark gray near to the view, and a light gray at the interior walls – to enlarge the feeling of space. The ceiling is built of thirty-six steel contoured structures, and covered by painted wood. The chairs and the wide windows are decorated in plant motives to enforce the connection with the surrounding scenery. When night falls, the lighting, which is between the ceiling beams, forms a warm and somewhat mysterious atmosphere.

VYTA – Boulangerie

Project Name: VYTA – Boulangerie **Designer:** Colli+Galliano Architetti **Location:** Rome, Italy
Photographer: Matteo Piazza **Area:** 150 sqm

This bakery was created inside a railway station, the modern symbol of speed and progress. The precise desire for integration and dialogue with the architectonic context is obvious from the very beginning. It shows that Vyta is totally projected towards the outside, and separated from it by a simple black portal. This was the theme of the interior design for the bakery, which starts from the traditional image of the bread shop; this is then reduced progressively to its essential features, in the quest for immediate and universal language that can guarantee the maximum usability in this place of transition.

The familiar colours of oak wood harmonize with the pale colours of the flooring and the ceiling, leaving space for monolithic furnishing accessories in black Corian that catalyze the attention through their symbolic purity. The polyfunctional counter is the heartbeat of every busy shop and in this case is used as an essential exhibition structure. There is a large decorative wall consisting of a paste creation symbolizing the surface and the fragrance of a bread crust.

In a delicate combination of prospects, the counter and the wall behind it curve towards the more intimate portion of the room, animated by tables and chairs submerged in a welcoming atmosphere and display alcoves similar to compact black boxes. There is also maximum design uniformity that slides unobtrusively into the busy station, while allocating ample room for the people waiting to depart, creating a relaxing ambience closely linked to the traditions that are hidden behind the minimalist lines — making Vyta a valid alternative to the world of fast food, and promoting good food culture.

EL JAPONEZ

Project Name: EL JAPONEZ   **Designer:** Cheremserran   **Location:** Osaka, Japan
Photographer: Cheremserran   **Time:** 2008

The floor of the restaurant is covered with a plastic carpet that evokes people of the tatami in Japanese architecture. The scarcity of columns is evident: only one column is clearly present in terms of space, which creates the impression that this long stretch is supported by only one structural element. There are other seven elements that playfully pretend to be columns but never touch the ground: they emerge from the soffit and have a specific role. The presence of wood as a material is not limited to the foreseeable use of floorboards, but contributes to the game of shapes and textures through the use of 10x10cm stud sections, which cover the solid sections and the soffit.

Over the bar, the stud wall shows some cavities, which are illuminated, making it appear less heavy and revealing that something happens behind them. A staircase hidden behind the bar leads to the rest rooms, which feature an opaque glass box contained in another wooden box. There, the environment is milder, and it playfully pretends to minimize the separation between the men's and women's rest rooms.

Charcoal BBQ 3692

Project Name: Charcoal BBQ 3692 **Designer:** studiovase **Location:** Seoul, Korea
Photographer: Park, Woo jin **Time:** 2007 **Area :** 248.7sqm

The designer has created the entire space with a keyword of "Layer originated from the Layer" of pork.
"Layer" means the section patterns of fatback. The fatback of pork most of Korean like has a layer of fat and a layer of meat again and again. This space shows that the layers are overlapped in many parts. Accordingly the designer has applied and repeated the "Layers" in this space. The shape of the furniture and lightings were designed one by one to express the concept. So are the repeated wires of the lighting and vertical and horizontal stripes of the furniture.
The designer has formed the layers by either using the grain of wood or piling up corrugated cardboard. The space is largely divided into the counter and waiting room, hall and kitchen. What is peculiar about this space is that the kitchen is so large to the extent that it occupies a third of the entire space. The space is warm, plain and subtle on the whole. Its feeling is a bit different and it breaks away from the typical image of the conventional restaurant. The designer painted pig-shaped objects and images, adding a sense of interest to the space.

Le Square Restaurant

Project Name: Le Square Restaurant   **Designer:** MOBIL M   **Location:** Nantes, France
Photographer: Florent Degourc   **Time:** 2006

Once upon a time there were two chefs who were also brothers. After opening two restaurants in Nantes, they decided to create a third one, close to the business quarters, therefore targeting a demanding clientele who often appreciates to be served in a rush but who still expects subtle and striking flavours as well as a well balanced wine list.
The Square offers indoor as well as outdoor meals. The outdoor space is also where ancient species of vegetables are grown for the restaurant's culinary purposes.
All the dishes are based on traditional French dishes, cooked with fresh ingredients and then enhanced with subtle flavours. In order to fulfil such a brief, a theatrical design approach was necessary: dishes are ordered, cooked and sent to the tables through an open counter that links the restaurant room and the kitchen. Pleasant cooking smells are hovering and open the appetite.

Sky 21

Project Name: Sky 21   **Designer:** Danny Cheng Interiors Ltd   **Location:** Macau China
Photographer: Danny Cheng Interiors Ltd   **Time:** 2007

This project brings a new challenge to the designer, to combine a bar, a dance club and a restaurant together in one place. Sky 21 is contemporary, minimal space with architectural forms combined.

On the 21st floor, a restaurant with a sushi bar is located at one end of the room. Semi-circular red sofas are cosy and better than having standard chairs and tables. Upon arriving on the 21st floor customers are welcomed by a black glass panel water feature stretching two floors. An outstanding effect is evinced when the adjacent colour changing LED-lit staircase connecting to the other floors like 22nd floor is seen through the water feature. The zone around the restaurant's sushi bar is capped with a low-lying black ceiling with exposed piping and lined with timber floors and black granite walls and mirrors and is separated from the VIP rooms with a UMU electrical semi-glass sliding door.

Upstairs, 22nd floor is designed as a two-zone bar, a separate lounge area and disco areas. This floor turns into a disco place filled with hopping dance music after 10 pm and different moment is functioned differently. On the 23rd floor, the roof, is a rest place for those who wish to take a break from pounding music and dancing. Placed with daybeds on a wooden platform, one feels like staying inside a relaxing lounge. A spacious outdoor wood terrace let customers enjoy the scenery of Macau, including the iconic Macau Tower and the ocean. There is the LED-lit dance floor with a commanding 9-LCD-panel graphic wall, the customer can relax and dance here. An open bar counter and a bed-seat area on an open wood deck is waiting them.

Kush 222

Project Name: Kush 222 **Designer:** Johnny Wong and Miho Hirabayashi **Location:** : Hong Kong Central,China **Photographer:** FAK3 **Time:** 2008

222 Hollywood Road is intended to be the flagship property for Kush and offers a full time concierge in the lobby. The entry signage is finished in black mirrored stainless steel and features LED lighting. With its 45 units, the open plan apartments each average 650 square feet. Designed with either a black and white or neutral colour scheme, they all include ebony hue hardwood flooring, Light Fantastic coloured mood lighting in a shelving niche behind the queen size bed and marble-clad bathrooms.

FAK3 designed a number of custom furnishing specifically for the site. Concealed within a cabinet are a dining table and two chairs that neatly fit together and can be whisked out for dinners at home. Black Nature is a custom floral arrangement or styling element that adds an ethereal focal point to the space. The China Dreams series of accessories including the gold magazine rack and table lamp are highlights in the living room. Meanwhile the bathroom includes an oversized sliding door that allows the entire bathroom to be completely open to the adjacent bedroom, exposing the shower within a glass box for added viewing pleasure. As its crowning glory, 222's roof features a lush garden with a Light Fantastic fireplace to take away the chill on romantic winter nights.

Chambers MN

Project Name: Chambers MN   **Designer:** Rockwell group   **Location:** Minneapolis , US
Photographer: Stuart Lorenz   **Time:** 2006

The concept for Chambers Minneapolis is a spacious residence for a collector of contemporary art. Cor-ten and blackened steel as well as sand-blasted stone clad the façade, while the interior features gallery-like white walls and floors of white terrazzo and ebonized wood planks.

The hotel has sixty guestrooms and special suites, including the "Rock Star Suite". Each room and suite has a minimalist, modern feeling: an open plan layout showcases carefully curated artwork, and a sleek bathroom includes an oversized shower and extensive counter-space. On the first floor, an intimate lobby-level lounge doubles as a breakfast room and a seating area. The first-floor public spaces feature contemporary artists' artwork.

The ground-level restaurant uses an industrial aesthetic: the stair is made of blackened steel and ebonized wood treads; original stone walls have been sandblasted and left natural; and custom lighting design reinforces the industrial motif. During the day, the restaurant is illuminated by a dramatic skylight. Chambers Kitchen also services the "outdoor living room" in the courtyard between the two wings of the hotel. Here, a giant gas fed fireplace is the focal point. At night, a large-scale video installation is projected on the building façade.

Carbon Hotel

Project Name: Carbon Hotel   **Designer:** PCP Architecture   **Location:** Brussels, Belgium
Photographer: Sita Tadema   **Time:** 2008   **Area:** 812sqm

The newly built Carbon Hotel and Wellness Experience is part of the vibrant rejuvenation of the commercial centre of Genk, the heart of the 19th-century Limburg coal-mining industry. The Carbon dedicates itself to life's vital element in both name and design.

The architecture office PCP developed both the building and the interiors, choosing materials based on carbon and the five basic elements – wood, fire, earth, metal and water. The facade is a succinct reference to the mining fields: jutting beyond the ground floor's wall of glass is a solid front of dark brown bricks that glisten in the sunlight. Creating another striking effect is the windows' asymmetric pattern: small square panes are recessed, while thin rectangular sections protrude as if clinging by magnetic force to the brick face. Interior walls have high-quality paints and wallpapers, which alternate matt and gloss finishes for a subtle contrast of texture and light.

Whether in the lobby lounge or in each of the 60 rooms, furnishings were selected for their honest use of materials: metal tables, wooden chairs, solid trunks as occasional tables, and fragments of stone. The use of indirect, coloured light in the rooms allows for easy adjustments to suit one's mood.

Klaus K Hotel

Project Name: Klaus K Hotel   **Designer:** SARC Stylt   **Location:** : Helsinki, Finland
Photographer: SARC Stylt   **Time:** 2006   **Area:** 1200 sqm

Inspired by the emotional contrasts of Finland's national epic, its nature and drama, Helsinki's Klaus K Hotel arrives bearing the stamp of Finland's finest architectural and literary traditions.

The Klaus K Hotel has transformed city landmark, formerly known for 65 years as the Klaus Kurki Hotel, with the help of major Finnish architects SARC Group and interior design by Stylt Trampoli. Located in the late 19th—century Rake building, the hotel brings Finland's national epic, the Kalevala, down to an intimate human scale throughout. The lead architects have created some of Finland's foremost modern architectural projects. Stylt Trampoli, led by Erik Nissen Johannsen, formulated the modern, contemporary inspiration of the epic implementing his craft into the hotel and restaurant design.

Each of the 137 guestrooms is given a theme illustrating the Kalevala's core emotional elements: Passion, Mystical, Desire and Envy. Klaus K aspires to go further rand "take the hotel out of the hotel": with the reception in the center of the lobby to tantalize and allure guests to visit its various food and drink atmospheres. Klaus K has created an ultradesigned life style experience where contrasts abound — Playfully delivering a luxurious experience of tradition and cutting-edge Nordic modernity.

The Dominican Hotel

Project Name: The Dominican Hotel   **Designer:** Lens Ass Architects   **Location:** Brussels, Belgium
Photographer: Lens Ass Architects   **Time:** 2007   **Area:** 1000 sqm

Tucked behind Brussels' famous theatre and opera house, The Dominican is a new hotel that offers a strong sense of history mixed with forward-thinking, eclectic design in the European Union's capital city. The hotel's sweeping archways are a clear reference to a Dominican abbey that stood on this site in the 15th century. Its original facade has been integrated into the new construction by the Belgian Firm Lens Ass Architects. Guests enter the lofty, high-ceilinged public spaces and their breath is taken away by the attention to detail. A stroll through the Monastery Corridor evokes an almost medieval feeling of elegance with original Belgian stone flooring. The Grand Lounge, considered the heart of the hotel, calls to mind the spirit of old European decadence in soaring windows and metalwork at the same time as attracting a definitively style-conscious modern clientele with its cutting-edge design.

The 150 guestrooms and suites – each with an individual look – are situated around a quiet inner courtyard and feature a rich combination of contemporary design and luxurious textiles, offering quiet comfort in a cloister-like setting. It's a wonderful respite from the Continent's new governmental hub, and a space in which old and new Europe effortlessly melds.

Jeronimos Hotel

Project Name: Jeronimos Hotel   **Designer:** Capinha Lopes& Associates   **Location:** Lisbon, Portugal   **Photographer:** Sofia Tavares   **Time:** 2007   **Area:** 1200 sqm

Where the tidal waters of the Atlantic flow into the estuary of the Tagus River, old and new come together in the hotel Jeronimos. Located in Lisbon's historic district and surrounded by museums and monuments, the 1940s building has been given new life by the Lisbon based architects Capinha Lopes & Associates, whose renovation of the hotel liaises with its surroundings. The ornate gables, statues and relief of the nearby 16th century Jeronimos Monastery accentuate the modern renovation. Windows afford a view of the monastery from the hotel's wine bar, where one can taste the rare and much sought, after Bussaco wine that has been produced for generations by the Alex and rede Almeida family, which also owns the hotel. As if to reflect the wines, the bar is designed in a rich savoury palette of red, white and brown, with a dark wood floor and floating lamps.

The welcoming reception desk — a lustrous, dark chocolate cube of wood before a crimson wall — greets guests in the same colour scheme. Each of the 65 rooms and suites has a pale marble bath room generously bathed in natural light. Throughout the hotel, the abundance of natural lighting blends the interior with the Lisbon sky outside.

The Levante Parliament

Project Name: The Levante Parliament   **Designer:** Michael Stepanek   **Location:** Austria, Vienna
Photographer: Michael Stepanek   **Time:** 2006   **Area:** 4600 sqm

The original building dates back to 1908, and is a perfect example of the Modernist architecture that was initiated by the Vienna School and Bauhaus. Its main characteristics, still evident today, are an emphasis on rationalism, the elimination of ornament and the use of technological advances in materials that allow for flexibility in design. This is the guiding principles by which the multidisciplinary team of architects, designers and artists transformed the building into an innovative space that integrates a gallery and the hotel. The glass design objects by artist Ioan Nemtoi have not only been given 4,600 square metres of prominent exhibition space, Nemtoi was also instrumental in the design of the restaurant and bar areas. The undefined borders between gallery and conventional hotel space have resulted in a challenging fusion of art and contemporary design.

The vision for The Levante's overall design concept is based on an interpretation of the four natural elements – transparency and light represent fire, the natural building materials symbolize earth, the generously sized rooms with 3.3 metres ceiling height stand for air, and the lineal forms and flexibility represent water. A range of core materials including light natural stone, glass, chrome and dark mahogany wood were selected to communicate the relationship to nature and harmonise with the classical modern design of the building.

CitizenM Hotel

Project Name: CitizenM Hotel **Designer:** concrete **Location:** Amsterdam, The Netherlands
Photographer: Ewout Huibers **Time:** 2008

Something exciting is happening in the world of hotels. A new type of traveller is walking through the door. These modern individuals are explorers, culture-seekers, professionals and shoppers. They travel a lot – both long and short haul. They are independent, sharing a respect for the places they visit and are young at heart.

The concept of the hotel is to cut out all hidden costs and remove all unnecessary items, in order to provide its guests a luxury feel for a budget price. The rooms are stacked on a ground floor with a dynamic lobby/living-room space, creating rooms and F&B functions. A red glass box with electronic sliding doors allows entrance to the hotel. The hotel does not have a service desk but a table with six self-check-in terminals. One of citizenM's hosts is present to guide you through the in check-procedure. The public area of the ground floor is divided in several areas to create a home-environment, by designing working areas, dining areas and sitting areas.

Murmuri Hotel

Project Name: Murmuri Hotel   **Designer:** Kelly Hoppen   **Location:** Barcelona, Spain
Time: 2008

Located in the emblematic Rambla de Catalunya, close to Las Ramblas, La Pedrera and surrounded by be best national and international boutiques, Hotel Murmuri offers those visiting Barcelona an incomparable accommodation choice.

The stone façade and the splendid windows of the building are in harmony with the typical architectonic style of the Eixample quarter. However, the interior has been designed in a wonderfully sober, pleasant and sensual fashion by the acclaimed British interior designer Kelly Hoppen who has managed to take care of every detail and to create a hotel with those personal touches that please even the most demanding and refined guests.

All 53 rooms have been decorated with an exquisite taste, meriting special mention the Suite with views over Rambla Catalunya and the Junior Suite. The combination of dark wood with various hues of beige, cream, grey and brown create a modern, contemporary and sophisticated atmosphere that will "age well".

Treading a thin line between modernity and tradition, Kelly Hoppen has made an intelligent use of neutral colours and rich textures managing to create a style that, though close to minimalism, it is luxurious enough to enchant even the most conservative guests. Her interior design projects have crossed international boundaries; she designed the Beckham's L.A house and even the first class cabins of British Airways.

From the moment a guest enters Hotel Murmuri, (s)he feels that (s)he is in the hands of professionals who not only respond to any of his/her needs, but who are also able to anticipate them. The hotel's team is young, dynamic, international and well trained to offer an excellent service: discreet, approachable and with an attitude and manners that will please even the most demanding guests.

Hotel Sezz

Project Name: Hotel Sezz   **Designer:** Shahé Kalaidjian, Christophe Pillet   **Location:** Paris, France
Photographer: Christophe Pillet   **Time:** 2005

What is it that your first experience at any hotel, no matter how fancy, makes you feel like you're waiting in line at a post office? In order to say no there is Hotel Sezz, which is why there is no check-in desk. When you entry, there is your personal assistant who will be just a phone call away for the length of your stay at the Sezz. You find yourself wishing they would stick around to give you a hand during your stay — making sure things run smoothly, getting you theatre tickets, going shopping with you to show you places not on every tourist map.

It embodies the designer's philosophy about what constitutes a luxury hotel in the 21 century. It's not about teak furniture, cashmere throws on the bed or hand-blown Murano glass flower vases. As it happens, the vases in the Sezz are hand-blown Murano glass. But as far as the designer is concerned, fine materials are just the opening ante to sit at the table. The smallest room is 200 square metres, and the larger ones are 400 square metres.

Running a luxury hotel, the designer promotes ease, comfort and unforced elegance and directed that most beds in the Hotel Sezz stand freely in the middle of the room, the easier to stroll around them. But really, the look of luxury is about a lot more than buying nice lamps and chairs. The trick is pulling everything together in a seamless whole.

The George Hotel

Project Name: The George Hotel **Designer:** synergy hamburg **Location:** hamburg, germany
Photographer: synergy hamburg **Time:** 2008

The George's unpretentious façade melds into the district's urban scene. Once inside, guests are warmly greeted by friendly staff and a welcoming atmosphere. "The design is meant to be fun", says Managing Director Kai Hollmann. "Stylistic contradictions here and there are absolutely intentional." The primary design scheme is held in black and white, yet the contrast is softened with warm dark woods and spots of colour. These heavier elements are skillfully balanced with gauzy fabrics, glass and an intelligent lighting design. Craftsmanship plays an important role in the interior design and handmade fabrics, carpets and unique pieces were selected by Hollmann during his travels.

A tour through the hotel is like a stroll through London: inspiring and visually varied. Exotic influences dating back to colonial times make a striking contrast to modern classics. Indian saris are colourful highlights as bedspreads while an oriental Marrakech style reigns in the spa. In the Library, modern interpretations of Chesterfield furniture, cosy niches as well as lavish carpets give the space a clubroom feel. It's the perfect spot to relax or read…and of course indulge in The George's own rendition of Afternoon Tea.

The hotel developer Kai Hollmann invests much dedication and commitment to his projects including sourcing unusual design pieces for his hotels through fine antiques dealers and specialist furniture boutiques.

Villa Florence Hotel

Project Name: Villa Florence Hotel   **Designer:** sfa design   **Location:** San Francisco, California
Photographer: Ken Hayden   **Time:**2008

Inspired by private homes in Florence and Tuscany, sfa sought to create a chic, modern design that would honor the most elegant, alluring elements of a traditional Italian villa. Mixing modern furniture with classic architecture, sfa design created a relaxing home away from home for anyone seeking a more personal escape in an expansive urban setting. Crossing San Francisco's swarming Powell Street, hotel-goers now meet an entrance of stone mosaic flooring and a rustic rock wall covered in ivy vines and an antique fountain. Stepping onto the Dijon-mustard, gold and cream terrazzo flooring of the foyer and greeted by an old painted mural of Florence, the ambiance is one of an expensive, yet intimate Italian home. Reinterpreted modern Italian art and contemporary velvet sofas adorned with colorful pillows invite guests into the warm living room of a private villa. Whimsical rugs and eclectic accessories from various antique stores and odd shops further this sense of an isolated Italian dwelling, always with a hip nod to the chic influences of modern boutique design. Clean-lined reception pods feature custom living glass panels lit from above to illuminate encased silk, vintage Italian scarves. The guestrooms are equally joyful and surprising in a palette of terracotta and celadon. Photographs of the familial scenes, modern art photography and landscapes give each room the feeling of home, while fun vintage images like that of Sophia Loren liven up the luxuriously modern bathroom.

JW Marriott Hotel Hong Kong

Project Name: JW Marriott Hotel Hong Kong **Designer:** JW Marriott Hotel Hong Kong
Location: Hongkong, China **Time:** 2007

Located near Hong Kong's International Airport and AsiaWorld Expo, the property's location gives easy access to the CityGate Outlets, Ngong Ping 360 cable car and the Tian Tan Buddha. Hong Kong's Central district is a 25-minute express train ride away.

The 658-room hotel is the only property in Hong Kong to offer guests golf packages with access to the adjacent SkyCity Nine Eagles golf course, and is the first to offer guests the territory's only Marriott spa, Quan Spa.

The façade flows with luxury to correspond to the flourishing context of the city. At the same time, the "luxury" concept continues in the interior — every element being meticulously selected and every detail being carefully handled. Comfort is another concept that the design concerns to ensure the guests a relaxing atmosphere. The bar in the hotel boasts sumptuousness and gorgeousness. The ceiling is dotted with "shining stars" with the beautiful chandeliers hang below, showing the "luxury" concept to the root; the seat made in unique shape also serves as decorative element. What more attracts eye is of course the lighting — shinning on the wine bottles.

The guestroom highlights comfort. The large French windows are specially designed from which natural light come in to render the whole room emerged in sunshine. Moreover, from here, one can fully enjoy the beautiful landscape outside. Moreover, the combination of red and white colours further enhances the concept.

Hotel Pirámides Narvarte

Project Name: Hotel Pirámides Narvarte   **Designer:** DIN interiorismo, Aurelio Vázquez Durán
Location: México City, México   **Photographer:** Jaime Jacott   **Time:** 2007

The main design concept was to create an oasis within Mexico City. The interior design is a retreat in where warmth and harmony are the leading characters of the ambiance. The hotel has 83 rooms and 10 different layouts were designed to have an interesting variety of regular rooms and suites. All the furniture is placed with a 30° inclination to avoid the monotony and interact with the different spaces that each room and suite has. Custom design art-object was designed and produced specially for each room. Wood frames with high resolution digital printed photographs of abstract parts of the human body hang from the walls and match with the tables that have the same kind of images.

Different levels generated by stairs and platform add dynamic to the rooms and empathise the different areas. The bed is always located in the centre of the rooms leaving the rest of the furniture to create the other spaces around it. Natural fiber hammocks, dinning room and a Jacuzzi with deckchairs complement the relaxing areas.

The lighting design was done with theatrical effects in mind. The combination of dimmers and different light temperatures create the atmosphere necessary for each activity while in the room. All the furniture and surfaces have a special UV coating for easy cleaning and maintenance. Bed covers and curtains were selected in a color scheme that includes: brick red, pistachio, cream and almond coffee. This colour palette is complemented with the natural materials and finishes of all the areas such as wood, granite and marble.

Mövenpick Airport Hotel

Project Name: Mövenpick Airport Hotel **Designer:** Matteo Thun & Partners
Location: Stuttgart, Germany **Photographer:** Matteo Thun & Partners **Time:** 2007

The way Mövenpick Hotel has been dressed up in grey pinstripe with touches of Prada Green provides that something extra perceptually speaking. Added symbolic value comes from the way the place is felt: airports are nodes on an international network, so the genius loci is a sort of national banner, not a local touch. The rooms in particular, provide places where guests retire, work on this assumption: it is the nation, not the city, which provides the most emblematic icons in a collage of images.

The Library

Project Name: The Library   **Designer:** Tirawan Songsawat   **Location:** Ko Samui, Thailand
Photographer: Tirawan Songsawat   **Time:** 2008

Distractions are kept to a minimum at this graceful hotel complex set in 6,400 square metres of lush Thai beachfront in Koh Samui. Group designer Tirawan Songsawat has created a minimalist structure, preserving a heritage property at the water's edge while intruding as little as possible on its ecology and aesthetics. The hotel's 26 suite-studio cabins are scattered discreetly around the ground. These consist of a ground-floor suite space and a separate studio upstairs that offers fabulous views of both ocean and old-growth trees that have been spared the developer's bulldozer.

Guests may lose (or find) themselves among vegetation interspersed with artwork and statuary, contrasting a bold colour scheme in which white, red, black and grey predominate: the Library's exterior is white, the swimming pool red, the restaurant grey. Interiors follow the same ultra minimalist palette and feature low-slung, rectilinear furnishings that invite visitors to stretch out and listen to the lapping of the waves — or of course dive into the books in the exemplary namesake library. Plasma-screen televisions and broadband connections complement golden Buddhas and wooden shutters in a perfect balance of nature, comfort and art.

Set on the beachfront area, the Page Restaurant and Bar provides an air-conditioned area and an open-air space overlooking the sea and the vivid red swimming pool. You can also relax on the wooden deck around the pool and restaurant area furnished with soft cushions and mattresses serving as sun loungers.

X2 Koh Samui

Project Name: X2 Koh Samui   **Designer:** Be Gray Limited   **Location:** Koh Samui, Thailand
Photographer: Be Gray Limited   **Time:** 2008

The X2 Koh Samui resort, pronounced "crossto", is intended for a cosmopolitan crowd eager to avoid the strict formality of traditional highclass hotels. Eager, that is, to "cross to" a whole new dimension of laidback luxury.

Beautifully located on Hua Thannon beach on the Southeastern coast of Koh Samui island, the newly-built resort offers twenty-seven villas resting on a largely undeveloped beach surrounded by old tree growth. The buildings' sleek, horizontally oriented design seems to meld into nature while its interiors in calm neutral tones stand in sharp contrast to the Gulf of Thailand's brilliant turquoise waters. Most of X2's villas have their own swimming pools and terrace gardens, set against a backdrop of swaying unspoilt palms. There is plenty to do and even excellent fusion food on offer all day at the resort's 4K (pronounced "fork") restaurant, but the resort's main activity is relaxation. For this reason, the huge outdoor massage pavilion probably best captures X2 Koh Samui's true essence. With just two beds on which to be pampered by expert hands, the coolly modernist building has an entire acre of land and thirty metres of beachfront to itself. This is a place to really feel that the most desirable luxuries of today are infinite time, endless space and sweet silence.

At 4K Restaurant, international executive chefs offer a wide range of fusion European and Thai dishes. The 4K restaurant and bar at X2 provide all day dining for guests between 7:00 am and 11:00 pm.

Thurles Arts Centre and Library

Project Name: Thurles Arts Centre and Library **Designer:** McCullough Mulvin Architects
Location: Thurles, Ireland **Photographer:** Christian Richters **Time:** 2006

In plan the building is similarly cranked, each zone mapped into trapezoidal volumes which master the bend of the river. In the library, a long thin space with its volume pressed to the river, a deep cut in the ceiling plane right through the research floor brings light and air to the centre of the plan at reading spaces and the issue desk. The exhibition space has a similar slice through the roof plane orthogonal to the first to conduct daylight through a huge roof light sitting across the upper terrace, giving unexpected views of the work on exhibition below. An introverted, reflective space, its walls splay out towards the riverfront, taking up the geometry of the site. Shielded behind the monolithic concrete entrance wall, the space can be glimpsed through a porthole when arriving, or alternatively closed off for hanging. The theatre foyer is similarly a compressed volume – vertical this time – caught between auditorium and boardwalk. Piercing the heavy concrete wall of the theatre, the control room is suspended over the café/bar. Large glass doors slide back to open the café and foyer to the boardwalk, and from the upper foyer the audience expands out on to the upper terrace overlooking the town.

Throughout the building colour is used to code and focus – red for information, orange for vertical circulation, white and black for concentration and relaxation. Seen from across the river these coloured zones resolve themselves into large scale gestures of connection in the case of tubes of orange stairs rising diagonally behind glass, intense dots of red marking out information areas, calm white zones of research and introspection, spots of black indicating more expansive night uses.

A.E. Smith High School Library

Project Name: A.E. Smith High School Library   **Designer:** Atelier Pagnamenta Torriani
Location: New York, USA   **Photographer:** Frank Oudeman   **Time:** 2008

The Alfred E. Smith High School building was built in the 1930s in Bronx as a vocational high school, providing its students not only with a high school diploma, but also with vocational skills such as building construction and auto repair. In fact, the school has gigantic car workshops. The project is the total reconstruction of an existing library space.

Public Schools in New York City are generally very large standardized brick buildings and have an average of 1100 students. The classrooms are situated along a double loaded corridor and the library space is part of the sequence.

The goal is to transform each new library into the school's living room.

A space that is enjoyed by the students, as well as the teachers and parents: kind of the heart of each school.(In fact, when the library had to be closed for the photographic shoot, the students, the teachers and even some parents asked to use the space.)

The designers incorporated into the existing room a floating element that modifies the library space perception and highlights the arts and crafts aspects of the school. The soffit is designed as a geometric progression: a double helix repeating modules of 12 triangular facets and defines the dynamics of the reading areas. The library-flooring pattern mimics the triangular progression.

Low open shelving separates the classroom, the lounge, and the computer area, leaving clear sightlines for the librarian. All furniture is modular, light and stackable; therefore, the space can morph from a classroom to an informal crescent layout to a formal meeting area for the teachers and parents.

Materials and finishes used in the project are environmentally friendly, recyclable and contain low VOC. With the aim of spending energy where it matters, Atelier Pagnamenta Torriani has put a good deal of time into public schools in order to provide quality for those who can benefit the most.

Wagner Middle School Library

Project Name: Wagner Middle School Library   **Designer:** Atelier Pagnamenta Torriani
Location: New York, USA   **Photographer:** Frank Oudeman   **Time:** 2007

The Wagner Middle School building was built in 1960 on the Upper East Side of Manhattan for junior high school students. The library space faces the playground and offers beautiful views of the townhouses along the street. The project is the reconstruction and enlargement of a library space.

The librarian requested shelving, a classroom, computer areas, a media centre, lounge area and a librarian desk. The designers manipulated the space by creating a series of waves, inspired by Hokusai's painting: Great Wave at Kanagawa. The soffit, the shelving and the floor pattern mimic the waves generating a spatial dynamic between the circulation and the reading areas.

The library is generally subdivided into four main functional areas: the greeting area with the librarian's desk, the computer area, the classroom and the lounge (chill-out) area. Low freestanding shelving units in the main library space define the various areas.

Lighting can be adjusted in each zone to create spatial effects, so that the users can emphasise one area or create a general subdued atmosphere when viewing a film. The graphics are designed with the principals and librarians. In the case of the vocational school, the principal desired a strong three dimensional soffit, rather than graphics.

Ps 11r Primary School Library

Project Name: Ps 11r Primary School Library   **Designer:** Atelier Pagnamenta Torriani
Location: New York, USA   **Photographer:** Atelier Pagnamenta Torriani: W. Tan, J. Son   **Time:** 2007

PS 11r is a primary school, built in 1919, in a middle class residential neighborhood in Staten Island, New York. It has beautiful large wood windows that allow natural light to penetrate deep into the classrooms. The library space is situated just above the auditorium roof and has unobstructed views to the green hills beyond.

A primary school library has to provide not only books and a classroom, but include space for the small kids to play. Therefore, the designers incorporated in the existing room an activity ribbon that separates the main shelving from the classroom. The activity ribbon provides a continuous lower area for the kids to sit and play, as well an area for the librarian. Above the ribbon, a deep soffit hides the air conditioning units. At both ends of the ribbon, two storage closets with a special whiteboard finish, provide a useful writing surface for fun activities. The open wood benches placed along the ribbon offer seating for the kids during the story hour.

Along the soffit, facing the classroom, the sentences from classic children books are playfully displayed while the names of the authors can be discovered at the back. The integrated shelving wraps around the whole room and has a spiral display section that from the lower level winds up to the top. The small classroom space is flexible and the light furniture can be re-arranged easily for parent-teachers meetings.

The Danish Jewish Museum

Project Name: The Danish Jewish Museum   **Designer:** Tomrerfirma Gert Fort A/S
Location: Copenhagen, Denmark   **Photographer:** Tomrerfirma Gert Fort A/S   **Time:** 2007

The architecture of the interior entrance space is meant to communicate the true importance of the museum. The visitor is drawn into the internal courtyard entrance, marked on both the horizontal and vertical dimensions. The horizontal space, or ground level of the entrance, is configured by an ensemble of conversation spaces developed into intimate meeting points for visitors and a space for an outdoor cafe in the summer months. The vertical walls are then marked by a projection of the Mitzvah configuration whose trace can be followed into the depths of the exhibition.

The organising principle of The Danish Jewish Museum is the concept of Mitzvah and its deep ethical meaning as a commandment, a resolve, and as a fundamental good deed. The museum takes the tradition of writing, reading and memory as the overall matrix of organising the exhibition space. In doing this, it is Mitzvah, on both emblematic and architectural levels, that guides a dialogue between the ancient vaulted space of the Royal Boat House and the walls of the Royal Library in relation to the experience of the new museum. To further emphasise this idea the entire exhibition space is illuminated by a luminous stained glass window that is a microcosm of Mitzvah, transforming light across the day.

Museum

Project Name: Museum   **Designer:** JSª   **Location:** Mexico City   **Photographer:** Jaime Navarro
Time: 2006   **Area:** 345 sqm

The building known as "La Esmeralda" in historic downtown Mexico City houses Carlos Monsivais' collection. The interior design of the new museum was entrusted to JSª (formerly Higuera + Sanchez). The building's architecture and the collection both are representative of Mexico City's history, and embrace periods from the Colonial times to present day.
How could the designers find the basis for such diverse subjects inside equally different environments?
The designers began with the entrance, where the intention was to capture the spirit of an "estanquillo" (neighborhood grocery shop), in an abstract manner, at the same time seeking to make it the "magic" door that would take the visitor on a trip to the past.
Climbing the staircase, you reach the first floor, which is a large open space, richly adorned with coloured moldings on the ceiling following the design of the cast iron. The furniture in the exposition must be silent, in face of a most eloquent architecture. It is white and formally independent of the environment. Nevertheless, it blends well with the warmth of the ornamental decoration, following soft curves it takes the visitor through the exhibit, where thematic niches are presented occasionally, like closed cells within the space.

New Acropolis Museum

Project Name: New Acropolis Museum   **Designer:** Bernard Tschumi Architects
Location: Athens, Greece   **Photographer:** Peter Mauss/Esto, Christian Richters, Bernard Tschumi Architects   **Time:** 2007

Program
With exhibition space of more than 14,000 square metres (150,000 square feet) and a full range of modern visitor amenities, the New Acropolis Museum will tell the complete story of life on the Athenian Acropolis and its surroundings.
Grounds
The Museum is surrounded by 7,000 square metres (75,000 square feet) of landscaped green space.
Amenities
The Museum offers a café overlooking the archeological excavation, a museum store, and a museum restaurant, with a public terrace commanding views of the Acropolis. The Museum is fully accessible to people with physical disabilities.
Principal Design Features
Designed with spare horizontal lines and utmost simplicity, the Museum is deliberately non-monumental, focusing the visitor's attention on extraordinary works of art. With the greatest possible clarity, the design translates programmatic requirements into architecture.
Organisation
The Museum is conceived as a base, a middle zone and a top. The base hovers over the excavation on more than 100 slender concrete pillars. This level contains the lobby, temporary exhibition spaces, museum store, and support facilities.
The middle (which is trapezoidal in plan) is a double-height space that soars to 10 metres (33 feet), accommodating the galleries from the Archaic to the late Roman period. A mezzanine features a bar and restaurant (with a public terrace looking out toward the Acropolis) and multimedia space.
The top is the rectangular, glass-enclosed, skylit Parthenon Gallery, over 7 metres high and with a floor space of over 2,050 square metres (22,100 square ft). It is shifted 23 degrees from the rest of the building to orient it directly toward the Acropolis. Here the building's concrete core, which penetrates upward through all levels, becomes the surface on which the marble sculptures of the Parthenon Frieze are mounted. The core allows natural light to pass down to the Caryatids on the level below.

The Art Institute of Chicago — The Modern Wing, Chicago

Project Name: The Art Institute of Chicago—The Modern Wing, Chicago   **Designer:** Renzo Piano Building Workshop, Paris, France   **Location:** Chicago, USA   **Photographer:** Dave Jordano **Time:** 2009

The new Modern Wing is being built between Michigan Avenue and Columbus Drive, at the northeast corner of the block the Art Institute of Chicago currently occupies. The addition will complete the cultural, urban campus of the museum. The new street-level entrance on Monroe Street will connect Millennium Park to the heart of the existing museum through the new Griffin Court. On the first floor, this daylit court will be flanked by new educational facilities, public amenities, galleries, and a garden, all of which will better actively link the Art Institute with urban life. The second and third floors will be dedicated to art and the viewing of art. The third floor will be completely lit by natural light. Below street level will be mechanical systems, art storage, and support facilities for the entire Art Institute.

Flying above the art pavilion will be a shelter that filters the sun to create the natural shaded light conditions ideal for the enjoyment of art. This shelter is a kind of flying carpet made of aluminum leaves that perform the same job as the tree canopies all around in the park. It is a "soft machine" that sensitively levitates above the new wing, vibrantly screening the light.

Limestone, a material used in the construction of the entire museum from its original Beaux Arts palace to recent additions, rises from the ground like a topographic relief, massive and solid, as though it has always been there. Above this topos, the building stands light, transparent, and permeable in steel and glass, in the great tradition of Chicago buildings: solid and robust yet at the same time light and crisp.

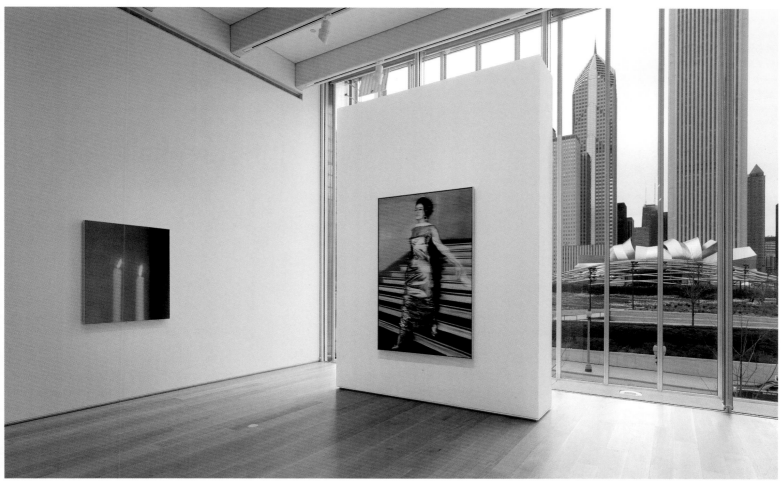

Arts of Asia

The Arts of Asia Gallery, Auckland

Project Name: The Arts of Asia Gallery, Auckland   **Designer:** Catherine Stormont, Nicole Pfoser, Gustavo Thiermann **Location:** Auckland, New Zealand   **Photographer:** HBO+EMTB   **Time:** 2008

The gallery is located in an existing exhibition space at the Auckland War Memorial Museum. The minimalist but finely detailed gallery showcases over 300 artefacts, providing built form that does not compete with the artefacts. The design team worked closely with the Gallery's curator to determine the most appropriate manner in which individual items are best presented, with consideration for chronology or theme.

Part of the challenge for the design and museum teams was to reduce it down to a manageable size to fit the exhibition space and still tell the story in a chronological sequence. The display cases need to sit within this space as a separate element but also needed to unify the space.

The concept for the gallery was to create a clean, linear and simple space which showcased the various pieces at their best while still keeping the valuable objects safe. In addition it was important to allow the audience maximum access to the pieces and for them to be able to get a close view if needed. Many of the pieces include intricate detailed work while others are large and need to be viewed from afar.

In order to enhance this it was decided that the cases should be constructed largely of glass creating an "invisible" barrier between the audience and the objects. Imperative to the aesthetic of the design was the visibility of the objects in the display cases. As few as possible "interruptions" in sight lines were needed which required the use of large glass panes which meant fewer joins. Innovative ideas were needed to support these large structures while still allowing the curators easy access to the objects for maintenance purposes.

Careful use of lighting was used to enhance the sense of drama and intimacy.

The desired aesthetic was to create a calm, tranquil space that allows the viewer to enjoy the individual beauty of the decorative objects while seeing them in the context of a historical timeline.

That's Opera

Project Name: That's Opera **Designer:** Atelier Brueckner GmbH **Location:** Brussels, Belgium
Photographer: Atelier Brueckner GmbH **Time:** 2006

200 Years of Italian Music
Temporary Exhibition
The opera is in the limelight. In celebration of the 200th anniversary of the music publishing
company Ricordi, the opera can be experienced from an unusual point of view. A red
carpet takes the visitors on a journey to the theatre's backstage world. They interactively
experience the genesis of an opera as a "Gesamtkunstwerk," or synthesis of the arts, step-
by-step in five exhibition cubes. They are present backstage when Libretto and Partitura find
their written expression, when stage design and costumes take form and eventually come
on stage for the performance.
Individually designed spatial narratives put the visitors in characteristic sceneries, for
example, Rodolfo's garret – inspired by the opera "La Bohème" – becomes the scriptorium
for the librettists in the first exhibition cube. In the following cube "Partitura", the visitors
enter an orchestra pit, where the instrumental parts are distributed on 42 directional
loudspeakers. The cube "Scenografia" takes them to the workshop of a stage designer, while
the setting of "Madama Butterfly" inspires the cube "Voci e Costumi". The latter is lined with
backlit Shoji wall elements reminiscent of Japanese architecture. At the end of their tour,
the visitors enter La Scala Theatre of Milan. Here, a 270-degree projection surrounds the
visitors with a contemporary staging of Aida: They can experience the opera from varied
and unusual perspectives, including from the stage.
The exhibition architecture follows the aesthetics of stage setting construction as well as
the materiality and degree of backdrop detail. The visitors are backstage in rooms that are
normally not accessible to them. Supports, wiring and spotlights are visible and arouse their
curiosity of the cubes' interior. These cubes are composed of one-metre-wide by three-
metres-high elements, which are shrouded with different materials. Thus, they can be
adapted to every location. The modular construction method allows for flexibility.

Bachhaus Eisenach

Project Name: Bachhaus Eisenach **Designer:** Penkhues Architekten, Kassel **Location:** Eisenach Germany **Photographer:** : Penkhues Architekten, Kassel **Time:** 2007

The Bach House in Eisenach, established in 1907 as a memorial for the composer Johann Sebastian Bach (1685-1750), is the starting point for admiration and research of Bach worldwide. The renovated and architecturally supplemented building ensemble was anew opened to the jubilee on the 17th May 2007. A new permanent exhibition, implemented by Atelier Bruckner in Stuttgart, puts the emotional, mental as well as musical potentials in Bach's work in the centre of the presentation. For the first time the sensuous experience of his creating is possible beside the mediation of biographic, historical and musical knowledge. A new building (after the plans of Penkhues Architekten, Kassel) offers the possibility to make the musical work of Johann Sebastian Bach learnable in its complexity and greatness. The new building closes a gap in the construction ensemble which exists of old building with cultivations, forecourt and bipartite court situation.

A diversified walk through the Bach House was established for the visitor. Through the entrance hall of the new building he reaches the historical old building where the history of the Bachgesellschaft, bearer and founder of the museum, is introduced and a music hall invites the visitors to linger. Valuable historical music instruments are not only shown here, but are explained and played every hour.

The upper floor of the old building is dedicated to the life of Bach in his historical environment. The new building provides the newest researches to the work of Johann Sebastian Bach and makes the musical experience very vivid. The individual elements of the exhibition design are employed very accurately, broken down and precise. Like a fugue of Bach, basic elements of the same kind in different variations are forming the spatial view. Referring to that idea only the materials aluminium and matt finished acrylic glass are employed throughout the exhibition.

Multikino Szczecin

Project Name: Multikino Szczecin   **Designer:** Robert Majkut Design studio   **Location:** Szczecin, Poland   **Photographer:** : Maciej Frydrysiak   **Time:** 2006

The project was to introduce Multikino to obtain cinema complex with unique and attractive character. The place which gives the viewers impression of peculiarity even before one enters the cinema hall.

Half-round and wide cash boxes perfectly introduced into the whole interior are one of the obvious stages. The assumption of main hall, particularly front well, was presenting the place of the cinema location as a part of the universal "world of the film".

Therefore, photographs of people resembling which are taken by paparazzi pictures of film stars are placed against a background of Earth, seen from the outer space. The viewer can not only watch a film here or stay in the interesting interiors, but also feel as a part of a film world, vibrant with activity, not only abroad in Los Angeles, London or New York, but in Szczecin as well.

The design includes a strong colour science fiction rather a sense of the future, as the audience entered the science fiction movies. The main colours of red, impressive and easy to create the feeling of excitement and happiness. The roof is black, the large spherical chandelier hanging in the air, like the shining stars in the night.

Blue Room Theatre at Chesapeake

Project Name: Blue Room Theatre at Chesapeake   **Designer:** Elliott+Associates Architects
Location: Oklahoma City, USA   **Photographer:** Scott McDonald, Hedrich Blessing   **Time:** 2007

The Blue Room is an element of Chesapeake Energy CEO Aubrey McClendon's overall goal to attract the corporation's next generation of accountants, engineers, geologists and technicians. McClendon's objective was to provide a multi-faceted centre that would enhance the workplace environment and provide greater employee benefit and retention.
The three-year design and development process of the Blue Room Theatre fulfilled this objective, culminating with a high end, cutting edge facility. The Blue Room Theatre is used for Chesapeake Energy's corporate meetings, videoconferencing, IT and operations functions, and geology and engineering department lectures. The Blue Room Theatre also serves as a movie theatre for employees during off-work hours.
The design takes advantage of the ascension/subterranean location to enhance an unexpected spatial experience; light and colour to create an immersive atmosphere; reflective, transparent, translucent and absorptive materials to create a superb acoustical environment; sound reflective blue cellular polycarbonate panel side walls which glow from backlighting; ceiling mounted MR 16 lamps containing clear and blue filters to provide white light for writing and blue light for atmosphere; dimmable room lighting settings for all white light, all blue light, combined colour and movie mode; and blue internal fiber optic glass column lighting.

Ordrup School

Project Name: Ordrup School   **Designer:** Bosch & Fjord   **Location:** Copenhagen Denmark
Photographer: Anders Sune Berg   **Time:** 2006

Based on the conviction that all people are different and have different ways of thinking and learning, at Ordrup School in Gentofte, Denmark, Bosch & Fjord have rejected the traditional design of school interiors and instead created varied rooms with space for differentiated teaching and creative thinking. The design is based on three key concepts: "peace & absorption", "discussion & cooperation" and "security & presence".

In the younger classes, peace and absorption are emphasised in the upholstered reading tubes, while movable pieces of carpet create temporary spaces for discussion and cooperation. In the mid-range age levels, the students can work together in smaller forums inside the sculptural Hot Pots or withdraw to the colourful concentration booths for concentrated reading and other work activities without being distracted by the surroundings. In the oldest classes, importance has been attached to the teenager's situation of being "on the way out into the real world". The bright red sofa islands on wheels can be moved around on the bright yellow floors and used for concentrated group work, loud discussions or movie showings. A long, bright green table sprawls through one of the rooms, forming a dynamic setting for creative cooperation and flexible work situations.

Medical Faculty, University of Groningen

Project Name: Medical Faculty, University of Groningen **Designer:** RAU
Location: Groningen, The Netherlands **Photographer:** Ben Vulkers Bjorn Utpott **Time:** 2008

Joined Movement
The Orthopaedic Institute wanted to erect a major building here to house its institute's rooms and a main lecture hall with space for 450 students and with a large foyer, connected to the institute's existing rooms. The new building would therefore have a "jointing" function in urban and programmatic terms as well.

Behind the glass revolving doors of the entrance area, facing the university plaza, an airy space is organised into 3 storeys developed, whose side walls partially consisted of the external walls of the existing developments. From the foyer, a single staircase leads to the two upper storeys, which house all the institutional rooms for orthopaedics. Within its two double arms, the first floor encircles an inner courtyard with garden, laid out on the roof of the lecture hall.

At the front of the foyer, a creatively designed concrete wall rises, which is the highest point of the giant lecture hall, half sunken into the earth. This wall, "Chromosome Technology in Concrete Relief", was designed in close collaboration with the artist Baukje Trenning. The lecture hall itself falls away towards a large white projection screen. Tables and chairs are combined to form a single large unit of furniture. They are sprayed red all over, a surface treatment technique borrowed from the motor industry.

A Skin of Gold
At the centre of the building is the concrete skeleton, a self-supporting column and ceiling construction. Steel "muscles" are connected to this "skeleton". This is covered by a gleaming golden "shawl", which spans the building. The double-curved aluminium "skin" melted so as to flow, involved a special craft technique. Multiply curving surfaces are not unusual on aeroplanes and ships. For this reason, a shipbuilder was recruited to deal with the statics. All of the double-curved surfaces which are also visible from the inside were made as prefabricated parts. The overlapping of the façade panels provides natural inlets fresh air.

Chesapeake Fitness Centre, East Addition

Project Name: Chesapeake Fitness Centre, East Addition   **Designer:** Elliott + Associates Architects
Location: Oklahoma City USA   **Photographer:** Scott McDonald Hedrich Blessing   **Time:** 2009

The Chesapeake Fitness Centre, East Addition is located on the campus of the Chesapeake Energy Corporation. The first Fitness Centre was constructed in 2003 and this is an expansion to that building. Headquartered in Oklahoma City, the company is the second-largest producer of natural gas in the nation and the most active driller of new wells in the U.S. The company's commitment is to encourage employees to live a healthy lifestyle, which is reflected in nearly every aspect of the campus. The fitness center, a 7,145,000-square-foot facility, embodies this by offering employees the ease of keeping fit without having to leave campus. Aerobics, cardio training, swimming, fencing, weightlifting, basketball and cycling are just a few of the programs offered under the guidance of an experienced fitness staff.

The designed addition is based on 'Jewel next to creek' concept. It is 1,450,906 square feet. The program requires that first, there should be three workout rooms. Second, there should be one regulation squash court. Third, there should be one additional basketball court with workout loft and last of all, the men's locker room should be enlarged.

Architectural Concept:

First, the glass workout tower with workout areas are transparent to campus but not to the public road.

Second, emphasising movement – people stretching in glass walkway and going up and down stairs are visible from public road.

Third, there is an articulate difference between structure and skin – glass is pulled away from concrete structure. The glass workout tower gives the feeling of being up in a tree house next to the creek.

14 Street Y Renovation

Project Name: 14 Street Y Renovation   **Designer:** Studio ST Architects   **Location:** New York USA
Photographer: Bilyana   **Time:** 2009

On the ground floor, the lobby, fitness centre, locker rooms, office, showers and pool are reorganised as a series of parallel bands. As users move through the different spaces, they experience the variety of happenings that animate the building.

The existing offices, which occupied the prime space along 14th Street, were relocated to make space for a new entrance lobby. This 469000-square-foot lobby has a gradient blue custom pattern cement tile floor, a field of circular fluorescent lights, and bright yellow 100% recycled plastic lounge furniture. New large windows were installed that open the lobby to 14th Street and bring the action of the street and natural light from outside into the space. A new garden was planted with colored pebble and birch trees to shade the facade. The overall effect is young, fresh and befitting the Y's East Village location.

The fitness centre, while not much larger than it was originally, now comfortably accommodates more fitness equipment. This space is also organised as a series of parallel bands corresponding to type of equipment (cardio, weight training, stretching etc.). The bright yellow and orange rubber floor brighten this windowless space. The waiting bench, fitness desk and low partition walls are all formed of curved rubber.

Locker rooms were relocated to the southern end of the fitness centre. The architects removed the existing vinyl floor and poured a clear layer of epoxy mixed with sand to create a slip-resistant concrete floor. The warm brown colour of this floor is juxtaposed with six vibrant colours of locker doors. Each colour indicates the type of locker, from monthly rentals to day use and handicap-accessible. The light fixtures, which are typical of construction sites and sidewalk scaffolding, float below the exposed concrete ceiling, creating a simple plane that complements the existing pipes and ducts servicing the upper floors.

Y+ Yoga Centre

Project Name: Y+ Yoga Centre **Designer:** Lyndon Neri and Rossana Hu **Location:** Shanghai, China **Photographer:** Derryck Menere **Time:** 2006

Y+ Yoga and Wellness Centre is an extension of the original Y+ Yoga Studio. The total area for this multi-purpose wellness centre is approximately 1200 m². The Centre, opened in December of 2005, contains three yoga rooms, massage rooms, meditation rooms, social gathering spaces, a small café, and a retail space.

The two internal yoga rooms have leaf patterns randomly placed on the walls and ceiling. One room has protruding light fixtures and the other has recessed light fixtures, creating a linear directional experience that emphasises fluidity. The third yoga room is a slightly elevated half-circular room in an abstracted forest clearing looking through the windows at a lake. The forest is abstracted with vertically hung ropes dyed in different shades of green representing a series of abstracted trees.

Additional rooms as part of the design serve to offer a complete oasis. The white room is an entirely white space from the ropes which hang from the ceiling, to the walls, floors, and cushions. The absence of colour allows an alternative space for self-reflection. The rooms for encounter are intermediary rooms that are strategically placed between the circulation and the yoga rooms. These spaces are for intentional and accidental encounters. Encounters between people are an essential part of human existence. These include rooms to cool down, rooms for reading, rooms to chat, rooms to settle down and rooms for meeting new people.

The bronze gaze holes, placed strategically throughout the space, allow the yoga performer to focus on a hole for various yoga positioning or posturing. From the corridors, the portholes also indulge the voyeuristic nature in all of us to gaze into a world of tranquility. This absorption of the world of tranquility into the "self" is initiated by the gaze-perception-sweeping out into the world.

Breaking New Ground

Project Name: Breaking New Ground   **Designer:** Jutta Friedrichs, Ben Houge
Location: Shanghai.china   **Photographer:** Jutta Friedrichs, Ben Houge   **Time:** 2008

100% Design Shanghai celebrates Shanghai International Creative Industry Week with the joint installation "Breaking New Ground," a collaboration between MÜ designer Jutta Friedrichs and sound artist Ben Houge, providing a sneak preview of next year's 100% Design Shanghai show. The 240 sqm joint installation provides a showcase for new local and international design objects, specially selected for the exhibition, which metaphorically break through the ground and float amid shards of ice, as a fresh wind blows in from overhead. This complete sensual experience reflects excitement and anticipation for the gathering wave of design and creativity that is swelling in China.
Designer Jutta Friedrichs and recipient of two Red Dot Design Awards this year, provides the vision behind the MÜ design furniture collection.

By studying our vast collections, Smithsonian scientists are [able]
to piece together the story of how insects and plants co-ev[olved]

Botany

Mission: To discover and describe the diversity of plants, explain how they evolved, and understand how humans affect and benefit from this diversity.

Collection: One of the ten largest in the world, with 4.7 million specimens representing all major plant groups and tens of thousands of species from all over the world.

Research: Fifty research scientists and affiliated staff focus on the origins, relationships, and classification of plants worldwide, especially the tropics.

Entomology

Mission: To discover, describe, and understand the diversity of insect species, which numbering up to 30 million, and of which fewer than a million have been identified.

Collection: One of the two largest in the world, with 35 million insect specimens from all over the Earth.

Research: Over 70 research scientists and affiliated staff from the Smithsonian Institution, U.S. Department of Agriculture, and U.S. Department of Defense collaborate to expand our knowledge of insects.

Paleobiology

Mission: To understand the history of life on Earth—how it has evolved, influenced, and responded to environmental changes.

Collection: The world's largest fossil collection, with some 40 million fossil plants, animals, and microscopic organisms that record the diversity of life over the last 3.5 billion years.

Research: Twelve staff research scientists and seven associates conduct research on evolution, biodiversity, climate change, and the interactions of life with geological processes, while 29 other staff oversee collections and assist researchers.

EXIT ONLY

← TICKETS

Butterflies + Plants

Project Name: Butterflies + Plants **Designer:** Reich + Petch Design International **Location:** USA
Time: 2008 **Client:** Smithsonian Institution National Museum of Natural History

In fall of 2007, the National Museum of Natural History opened a new Butterflies+Plants: Partners in Evolution exhibit set within the context of exhibits explaining the co-evolution of butterflies and plants. Reich+Petch Design International was responsible for the conceptualization and design of all exhibits inside the Pavilion and in the surrounding Hall. The firm worked closely with the museums' scientists and writer to develop the narrative sequence. Reich+Petch Design International also worked closely with the architectural firm responsible for the Pavilion shell structure to ensure efficient visitor flow and seamless integration of displays and environmental support systems.

The concepts were inspired by the colours and forms of the beautiful content and played with scale and imagery to create a delightful experience of fun exploration. The space planning and details were designed to accommodate the museums' exceptionally high numbers of visitors (several millions per year). The exhibit surrounds the visitor with colourful arrays of imagery and specimens to reinforce the connection between evolution and diversity.

Metamorphosis:

Foes. . .

Transform to. . .

Evolving Together

Butterflies and plants interact with each other — sometimes as friends, sometimes as foes.

Fuji Xerox Epicenters

Project Name: Fuji Xerox Epicenters   **Designer:** Geyer Pty Ltd   **Location:** Sydney, Tokyo, Singapore And Shanghai   **Photographer:** Tyrone Branigan   **Time:** 2007   **Project Size:** 5000-8000sqm

Geyer were commissioned by Fuji Xerox, in collaboration with Landor brand and graphic consultants, to create four customer innovation centres across the Asia Pacific to celebrate the heritage brand and reinforce their leadership position in the digital production print market. These "Epicentres" are located in Sydney, Tokyo, Singapore and Shanghai.

The vision of the centres is to offer Fuji Xerox's global customers a complete "digital print" experience – with a focus on business solutions not just "hardware"/equipment.

Visitors are provided with a personalized journey depending upon the reason for their visit and the level of existing knowledge of the Fuji Xerox products and services. A series of "experiential zones" are personalized for each customer, ensuring relevance of brand communication through to sales conversion and customer retention experiences.

From arrival the customer's experience is extraordinary. An iconic sphere, projecting welcome messages to the customer, denotes the entry point. Visitors are greeted by a roaming attendee, unrestrained by the confines of a reception desk. The traditional reception zone has been replaced by a dynamic Fuji Xerox brand "Immersion Zone" where visitors are subliminally immersed into the total brand experience through sound and video content.

Stylecraft Showroom

Project Name: Stylecraft Showroom   **Designer:** Geyer Pty Ltd   **Location:** Sydney, Australia
Photographer: Andrew Sheargold   **Time:** Sydney 2007   **Area:** 500-600 sqm

Stylecraft is a leading provider of high quality commercial, hospitality and residential furniture to the architectural and design community, representing original contemporary design from Arper, Akaba, Bonestil, Cornwell Hecker, Dynamobel, ESO, Parri, Stua and Verzelloni.

Stylecraft wanted to create a dynamic and innovative space that draws customers to the showroom — and encourages them to return.

Geyer's design solution embodies Stylecraft's brand attributes – energetic, confident, kinetic and fun.

The space has been designed to evolve and change with the business, and enables a diversity of customer experiences. A highly flexible environment has been established that allows the space to constantly evolve and change to support a range of local and international brands and new product lines.

Two key environments have been created, the showroom and sales work area. While there are no walls separating these areas, the use of different finishes and lighting dramatically affects the mood and creates a clear distinction between the spaces.

In a move away from the traditional "chair wall", mobile chair towers are suspended from the ceiling and slide effortlessly through the showroom. This gives the chairs (Stylecraft's core product offer) prominence within the space. The mobile towers also allow the space to be quickly and easily reconfigured to cater for Stylecraft product launches and industry events.

Haloid 3

Bernhardt Design Showroom

Project Name: Bernhardt Design Showroom **Designer:** Lauren Rottet, Kelie Mayfield, Christopher Evans **Location:** Chicago, USA **Photographer:** Eric Laignel **Time:** 2008

The Bernhardt Design Showroom recently moved locations within the Chicago Merchandise Mart in May 2008 to the opposite side of the building, down the hall from the previous showroom. The move created a challenge for the design team since the new space no longer had the wonderful views of the river and the showroom decreased considerably in size to only 7,000 square feet. This move caused a significant challenge to adequately display the client's furniture product. The design team's solution was to create a space that would emulate a museum setting for the furniture to be displayed as art.

The biggest challenge the design team was charged with was to create a small space that feels much larger than its actual size. The design team utilized light as the medium for solving this challenge and the source for extending the perception of space. Light was used so that solid planes never touch floors, walls or ceilings and always have the appearance of floating. Light paneled walls were also used as accents to reflect light so as to create the appearance that natural light leads one into the space beyond — as if the front door was opening and allowing daylight to enter the space.

The space also had no interesting views to the outside world so the design team decided to create a world inside the showroom and focus the attention of the viewer on the art — the furniture. The design team's solution was to create an ephemeral wall which would also double as a backdrop for the client's chair display. The wall is comprised of metal painted white with a custom designed perforated pattern. Fabric scrim was stretched behind the panels to wash the light fixtures and create a consistent source of light. The floor pad aligning the paneled wall is made up of shiny white epoxy resin to help reinforce an idea of a plinth, but yet accessible and inviting for one to experience the chairs and become part of the art scene and experience.

The finishes used in the space also played a significant part in the overall design. The materials used in the architecture and furniture are all "visually quiet" to not interfere with the lines and detailing of the furniture. The space is void of colour and the fabric and carpet used hints at the idea of wool or cotton before it is dyed and coloured.

BRANCH in Changchun

Project Name: BRANCH in Changchun   **Designer:** Keiichiro SAKO, Yoshimasa TSUTSUMI/SAKO Architects   **Location:** Changchun, China   **Photographer:** Misae HIROMATSU (BEIJING NDC STUDIO, INC.)   **Area:** 280 sqm

One corner of the Changchun Library of Jilin Province is a culture exchange centre founded by International Exchange Foundation that devoted to introduction of Japanese culture to Chinese people. In order to create a relax space with easy access to people for party or personal ease, where they can find their respectively satisfactory and pleasant things, the designers designed it by centring on trees. Any designs in the room are characteristic of a forest, attracting and charming, with people seating or leaning on the branches and hiding between branches. It is a space that arouses people's imagination.

The complicated design at first sight is factually based on human structure, including davenport, sofa and desk, all much convenient for people. The material adopted is the high-dense plate and is assembled at the site after rough preparation in Beijing. It has fully reflected the highly efficient construction management and operation. The floor, wall and ceiling are generally white and the original pillar is covered with stainless steel mirror to weaken its existence. The design, green in general, gives relaxing touch to the whole space and the color gradation, together with the LED lamp, has made much of its vitality. Besides, sphere-shaped LED lamps are also placed everywhere in the room to convey the morning dews impearled on leaves.

It is a place full of vines and tendrils that produces diversified achievement and it is an organic and complimentary unit formed by inter-twisted vines. The division and unity of the tree have just depicted the exchange and growth of the relationship between China and Japan.

FlatFlat in Harajuku

Project Name: FlatFlat in Harajuku   **Designer:** Keiichiro SAKO, Yuichiro IMAFUKU / SAKO Architects
Location: Tokyo, Japan   **Photographer:** Chikao TODOROKI / Sasaki Studio Inc.   **Time:** 2008
Area: 328 sqm   **Client:** NHN Japan Corporation

FlatFlat in Harajuku is the store where the visitors are actually able to experience Hangame, an online games portal, and Hange.jp, a games portal for mobile phones, developed by NHN Japan Corporation. Located at the centre of Harajuku, the store occupies a narrow space of 3.5 metres wide by 45 metres long. The concept of the store is the future park and the designers attempted to combine virtual element with real space opens to anyone. It is not only the space where 'organic principle' and 'inorganic principle' stay together, but it represents the modern society consisting of real and virtual environments.

"Organic principle" consists of curved lines and has a space characteristic of a cave that people can discover depending on each purpose and feeling while the different scenes unfold continually. They attempted to create a space that people feel like snuggling up to the organic form that curves based on human body dimensions. Visitors do not hesitate to enter the store because of the sense of closeness. On the other hand, "Inorganic principle" consists of white wall surface fixtures, neon tubes of ceiling illumination and mortar floor creates virtual character. They also used the lines which let neon tubes and the prevention of crack seam of mortar offset the forms of the wall surface fixtures. They stimulate curiosity of the visitors by synergy with the forms of the fixtures and lead them to the inner part of the narrow space.

homeculture

Project Name: homeculture   **Designer:** Franken Architekten   **Location:** Berlin, Germany
Photographer: Franken Architekten   **Time:** 2005

The designers would like to provide a spatial context for the entrepreneurial vision of the client – visible, tangible, and palpable to all the senses. They are never just functional, but rather communicate and transport messages effectively and intuitively.

So they present the designers a showroom like a high-end fashion store for a selection of tiles and spa assecoires.

The store provides an ideal presentation platform for Raab Karcher and its four joint-venture partners from the premium tile and bathroom fittings sector.

The designer used animated lines of vision in order to generate virtual space.

As the onlooker's gaze wanders along the front was taken as the basis for generating the interior's geometry by means of computer simulation. The fact that it is shallow in depth means that for passers-by the store functions as an elongated shop window.

Visual-kinetic installation is another feature of this project.

The Liquid Wall appears like a vertical water wall and serves as an eye catcher in the Ku'Damm facade. In a computer simulation, the passer-by's gaze causes an acrylic glass pane to vibrate.

The frozen vibration acts like a distorting lens and makes the illuminated back wall oscillate as you wander past it

GRAFTWORLD-Exhibition in the Aedes Gallery

Project Name: GRAFTWORLD-Exhibition in the Aedes Gallery   **Designer:** Graftlab
Location: Berlin, Germany   **Photographer:** Jan Bitter   **Time:** 2007

In addition to GRAFT's the widely published projects, like the prize-winning Hotel Q in Berlin, Restaurants Fix and Stack in Las Vegas and several international houses, the exhibition will focus on the new and unpublished work of GRAFT, including numerous highrise buildings, special hotel designs and private residences, research installations as well as public projects.

GRAFTWORLD refers to GRAFT's specific method of work process, which fuses syntactic, semantic and phenomenological aspects into architecture. GRAFT uses narrative elements of cinema, exploiting space — time interconnections through storyboarding with progressive technical research of long term collaborations with various companies.

The exhibit showcases this methodology in an accessible, usable exhibition sculpture, an interactive lounge displaying projects of all three office locations. Classical distinctive architecture elements like floor, wall and ceiling as well as the classical disciplines of additive plasticism and substractive sculpture will be fused into a lounge-display-hybrid. GRAFTWORLD is thought to be inclusive and rather crosses and blurs boundaries than accepting their exclusive nature.

GRAFTWORLD proposes architecture that can evolve to be sculpture, be furniture, be a product, be an urban scenario, be landscape at the same time. Design, methodology and technology are not classically "displayed", but are integrated in the GRAFTWORLD .

NETWORK SHOWS

SELECT SHOW
SIMPSONS
FAMILY GUY
LAW & ORDER
AQUA

Moonraker

Project Name: Moonraker   **Designer:** Graftlab   **Location:** Burbank USA   **Time:** 2006

Graftlab will design and build these worlds as stages of visual communication. Like a set design, these interior worlds will be erected within a hangar or loft space. They will become accessible statements, places of experimentation and inspiration.

Concept

To provide a tangible, engaging experience representative of future Volkswagen customer needs and desires, an advanced look at themes will be of growing importance in the coming decade. The Life Settings will be a powerful tool to support and inspire a multitude of projects. Four futuristic scenarios illustrate a broad spectrum of user types, interests, competencies and aesthetics.

Aspirational architecture will showcase forecast technologies and concepts in a progressive sequence, preceded by a walk through the current consumer kit presentation and finishing with an automobile sized viewing "drive way". The installation can be modified to suit a variety of foreseeable scenarios and uses.

Internorm Flagshipstore

Project Name: Internorm Flagshipstore   **Designer:** ISA STEIN Studio   **Location:** Pasching, Austria
Photographer: TEAM M/ISA STEIN   **Time:** 2007

The Frame
Unique in its design and grace, the "archi-FRAME" from Internorm is setting new standards in the architecture of a CI-suitable Flagship-Store. The frame is an integral part of Internorm's "corporate identity" – the company identity. One can look into the showroom via the building-high "archi-FRAME". Thus the showroom itself is presented through a larger frame as is the production of windows and the shell which would otherwise play a secondary role.
The "archi-FRAME" is made of coloured glass and thus establishes a relationship to the main material of the windows. The glass is used here as a constructional element and not as a filling as is normal. During the night the lettering INTERNORM is illuminated on the frame which is likewise lit up.
Insights, Views, Openings
In the interior, the views and insights were of particular importance to the Architekten Team. In particular a visual contact was to be established to the showroom from the first floor. Thus one can look from the kitchen or the meeting room through a belt of windows into the sales room.
Apart from the frame, the core of the company, the use of images was also important. The aim was to liven up the room via a wall projection. Thus various subjects from Messrs. INTERNORM find a place in the showroom. The images are also to be found in a niche with a seating arrangement and in the conference room.

Heaven

Project Name: Heaven   **Designer:** Capella Garcia Arquitectura   **Location:** Barcelona Spain
Photographer: Rafael Vargas   **Time:** 2008

"Heaven" invites the visitor to travel along a tunnel revealing the material's varied possibilities. There are two openings in the facade: one of them, which comes forward to receive you, is the entrance, and the other, which seems to retreat from you, is the exit. The interior lighting keeps changing colour and shade, making the plastic membrane into something living. As you enter you go through a large dome where an oscillating lamp hangs like a tonsil. In one place, the glossy-finish plastic material looks like a painted wall and reflects the light; in another, the same material, but this time with a translucent finish and illuminated from behind, turns the walls into a great lamp that keeps taking on different colours, through a system of electronically-programmed LEDs. When you reach the end, the black walls make the space disappear, and in the darkness the moving image of a fire emerges and vanishes behind the microperforated surface of the material, deceiving the eye and producing a hyper-realistic effect. Opposite the image, in the central zone, one whole wall is filled with a projected video of the sea-bed in constant motion, giving the sensation of being submerged under water. Continuing towards the exit you come to an oval window where the material becomes semitransparent, and through it can be seen a curtain of autumn leaves in silhouette, in constant movement thanks to a fan.

It has been like a journey through an organic space, a series of parabolic, warped shapes that would be impossible to make in any other material. When it is taken down, the entire installation will fit into a small, light case. This plastic material avoids the need to build walls and ceilings with plaster and paint, requires practically no maintenance and is very quick to install. Its lightness means that it is easy to transport and it is totally demountable and recyclable. All in all, it is a good option for ecodesign and sustainability.

Tesla Store

Project Name: Tesla Store   **Designer:** CCS Arhictecture   **Location:** Los Angeles, USA
Photographer: Eric Laignel   **Time:** 2008

Tesla Motors, maker of the world's most advanced electric car, has opened its flagship Los Angeles location, featuring architecture by CCS Architecture, in May of 2008. Like Tesla's electric sports cars, the store design emphasises style, efficiency and performance.
Located on the corner of Santa Monica and Sepulveda boulevards, the $2 million dealership sprawls 10,000 square feet and features poured concrete floors, an exposed ceiling of ductwork and beams, mirrors and potted plants.
CCS has merged to create an efficient, gallery-like setting for showing and servicing the cars. "The cars are beautiful, so the showroom is set up to be a boutique experience, where the intended rawness of the space counterpoints the sleek refinement of the cars. It's like sculpture in a gallery," says Smith, a car dealerships. The design unifies the showroom and service areas, making the service process fully transparent to guests as well as passersby on Santa Monica Blvd. With an electric car, there is no noxious smoke, no puddle of oil or gasoline, and no loud engine. The Tesla mechanic, like a chef in an open kitchen, has nothing to hide.

ProNature

Project Name: ProNature   **Designer:** Joey Ho / Joey Ho Design Ltd   **Location:** Elements, Kowloon Station, Hong Kong   **Photographer:** Ray Lau   **Time:** 2007

The design of the first "ProNature" outlet for Asia's leading healthcare company Eu Yan Sang applies the traditional Chinese philosophy on natural phenomena, "Wu Xing". The five elements: metal, wood, water, fire and earth, have been carefully applied and interpreted in a modern sense and manner to demonstrate the brand's mission of "caring for mankind".

The design aims to regenerate Eu Yan Sang's new product line and its core focus in traditional Chinese medicine into a new and fresh image. Graphics generated from herbs related to the five elements are used on the wall and ceiling feature respectively, and two trees are planted from floor to ceiling at the shop front that serves as both a loose screen and an attractive product stand. As the name of the shop suggested, natural elements are emphasised in the whole design of ProNatural. Natural colours with warm lightings create a natural and fresh atmosphere that act as an act-on and tone up with the image of the brand and it's products. All in all, the ProNature shop presents a young and refreshing image that change people's preconceived idea towards Chinese herbs and supplements, paving new acceptance of Chinese herbs especially among the teenagers.

Healthy Life Natural Health Food Store

Project Name: Healthy Life Natural Health Food Store   **Designer:** Design Clarity
Location: Sydney, Australia   **Photographer:** Design Clarity   **Time:** 2007

Healthy Life offers a wide variety of natural health and beauty products, vitamins, minerals and sports supplements. Having built a reputation as the leader in the health sector, Healthy Life required a new, invigorated store design to reflect the quality of their product ranges.
The design brief was to develop a memorable, new identity for Healthy Life including 2D graphics, 3D environmental branding, packaging, uniforms and a full store design concept that could be easily adapted to a wide variety of sites throughout metropolitan and regional Australia. Inspired by nature, Design Clarity developed a brand icon based around the tree motif. Crisp, green colours were specified to evoke a feeling of energy and well-being, while raw-looking finishes were adopted to reflect the honest, natural feel of the brand.
Ceilings and services are left exposed and sprayed out black as a backdrop to the basic white, green and timber palette. Adaptive re-use of familiar, natural, and earthy materials in new and less predictable ways engages the customer and allows for an environmentally aware approach to the design.
The entrance of the store features a striking timber slat shopfront that frames a glass window display, providing opportunity for dynamic visual merchandising and seasonal product displays. A bold ceiling feature draws customers into the space and departmental suspended chalkboard signage blades throughout the store facilitate easy navigation.
Market-style merchandising units including baskets, ladders and timber crates are included to allow each franchisee to create feature displays to suit their individual store requirements. Materials such as natural pine timber, zinc plated steel, chalkboard, polished concrete tile and simple pegboard are used to reinforce that familiar, comfortable and environmentally-friendly look and feel.

Barbie Shanghai

Project Name: Barbie Shanghai   **Designer:** Slade Architecture   **Location:** China, Shanghai
Photographer: Iwan Baan   **Time:** 2009

The 35,000-square-foot Barbie Flagship for Mattel holds the world's largest and most comprehensive collection of Barbie dolls and licensed Barbie products, as well as a range of services and activities for Barbie fans and their families.

Mattel wanted a store where "Barbie is hero", expressing Barbie as a global lifestyle brand by building on the brand's historical link to fashion. Slade Architecture were charged with the design of everything. Barbie Shanghai is the first fully realised expression of this broader vision. It is a sleek, fun, unapologetically feminine interpretation of Barbie: past, present, and future.

The façade is made of two layers: molded, translucent polycarbonate interior panels and flat exterior glass panels printed with a whimsical lattice frit pattern. Mattel collaborated with designers at BIG, the Branding and Design division of Ogilvy and Mather, who created the final exterior frit graphics. The two layers reinforce each other visually and interact dynamically through reflection, shadow and distortion.

For the new façade, they combined references to product packaging, decorative arts, fashion and architectural iconography to create a modern identity for the store, expressing Barbie's cutting-edge fashion sense and history.

Upon entry, visitors are enveloped by curvaceous, pearlescent surfaces of the lobby, leading to a pink escalator tube that takes them from the bustle of the street, to the double-height main floor.

The central feature within the store is a three-storey spiral staircase enclosed by eight hundred Barbie dolls. The staircase and the dolls are the core of the store; everything literally revolves around Barbie.

The staircase links the three retail floors:

The women's floor (women's fashion, couture, cosmetics and accessories). The doll floor (dolls, designer doll gallery, doll accessories, books). The Barbie Design Centre, where girls design their own Barbie is on this floor. This activity was planned by Chute Gerdeman Retail and designed by Slade. The girls floor (girls fashion, shoes and accessories).

WEEKDAY MALMÖ

Project Name: WEEKDAY MALMÖ   **Designer:** Electric Dreams   **Location:** Malmo, Sweden
Photographer: Fredrik Sweger   **Time:** 2006   **Area:** 1000 sqm

Weekday is a visionary, young clothing company. It has grown rapidly from being a small hobby project, open on weekends only, to five full-size stores, much thanks to their Cheap Monday success. The retail chain has, along with Monki, recently been sold to H&M. Weekday wants to grow without repeating itself. They want each of their stores to be unique and every project starts as a blank canvas.

A 1000-square-metre fashion store in central Malmo opened on October 26th 2006. The entrance level hosts in-house jeans brand Cheap Monday and top floor contains Swedish and international designers, second hand garments, and shoes. The top floor also houses a screen-printing studio, a fully equipped industrial laundry for dying jeans, a DJ stand, and a sewing studio.

The designers like to think of interiors as landscapes and structures. At a first glance, the interior is a maze. The angular mirrors are creating spatial confusion. It's skewed and chaotic, lots of edges and corners. But as soon as you start to explore the shop you realise that all functions are seamlessly integrated and that the green ramps form a distorted honeycomb grid that is projected on the inner ceiling. The structure is creating a non-linear flow, an unusual way of moving in a shop. There is no obvious route from dot A to dot B. It's a scripted journey from folded jeans to shoes to fitting rooms to checkout.

They think of the store as an abstract tree, with its supporting root system at the Cheap Monday level and its branches being the chrome-plated giant clothes hangers at the external designers' level, all with a pinch of disco flavour.

Monki Stockholm

Project Name: Monki Stockholm   **Designer:** Electric Dreams   **Location:** Stockholm, Sweden
Photographer: Fredrik Sweger   **Time:** 2007

Monki is a new chain of fashion stores for girls, carrying its own moderately priced clothes line as well as selected designer brands. The Monki concept is based around a story about a world of creatures; hatched from chimneys, grazing sea shells. The Monkis dwell in a world made up of both the magical and the ghastly. The Peacock Fields, the City of Oil and Steel, and the Rosehip River are all landmarks in this suggestive scenery. When you walk into the store's abstract forestlike landscape, you step into a part of the Monki World.

The interior is an attempt to add to the myth of this mystic being. Details and references are to trigger imagination; entering a fitting room is stepping into a hollow oak, clothes rails are glowing tree branches, and accessory displays are shiny chrome-plated mushrooms. The Monki character is not only featured in logos, printed patterns on garments; it is also represented as stuffed animals. To create a flexible, detached world adjustable to any given store layout, a catalogue of modular key elements was designed: the Monki Alphabet. The basic grammar for this scale 1:1 Lego is a c/c 1200 modular sequential system of loops. Every loop is an unbroken line, a dissolved horizon where the floor climbs up on the walls and the ceiling reaches down to meet the floor. The elements can be combined in numerous ways within each loop, to 3D-transform generic retail space into a highly differentiated spatial experience.

In its first year, Monki opened 11 stores throughout Sweden, challenging the notion of generic low-price fashion retail with an exclusive boutique-style interior. Monki rather puts their marketing budget on a high profile store design than on full-page spreads in local newspapers. The Monki Götgatan store was the seventh in the Monki 1.0 series and opened in late March 2007. The current concept is the three-dimensional interpretation of the Monki Wetlands. Next years' establishments will feature another place in the Monki World: Monki 2, the City of Oil and Steel, an all-new interior concept.

MONKI 1: Forgotten Forest

Project Name: MONKI 1: Forgotten Forest   **Designer:** Electric Dreams
Location: Linkoping, Norrkoping, Stockholm, Vaxjo, Eskilstuna,Gothenburg, (Sweden)
Photographer: Fredrik Sweger   **Time:** February 2008- March 2009

Once upon a time, an unexpected chemical reaction in an old weavery released a batch of plump black Monkis into the sky. Soaring high from the still-smouldering chimney, the tiny creatures floated into the illusory universe known as the Monki World. Appearing simultaneously with the Monkis was a new fashion label and a retail concept for girls; combining graphics, goods, and store design to form an overall story. When you enter a Monki store, you step into a part of the enchanted Monki World.

The Monki World is a story about a parallel universe inhabited by little black creatures with dual personas, born in the derelict City of Oil and Steel. Monkis are cute and friendly, but also evil and deceptive. Their world is made up of places as surprising and ambiguous as themselves; part magical and part ghastly; stunning beauty alongside revolting ugliness.

This story is the foundation for Monki's all-embracing retail concept. The story is not only communicated as printed patterns on garments, graphics, websites, and store designs; the Monki World is represented even in the smallest details, such as accessories, shopping bags, price tags, and receipts.

Monki has several interior concepts running simultaneously. Every concept is inspired by a different part of the Monki World. So far, the mysterious Forgotten Forest and the powerful City of Oil and Steel have been launched. Future concepts will portray other areas of the vast Monki landscape. Ultimately, all the stores together form an entity that combines recognition, repetition, and surprise.

The all-new concept for Monki, "the City of Oil and Steel," is a surreal world full of chemical left-overs, broken skyscraper parts, and giant beaded necklaces. The floor is glossy black flowcrete, like wet neon asphalt. The wall interior is an abstract collage-city of broken skyscraper parts of different scales. The walls are completely mirror-clad, creating an illusion of horizontal and vertical free-floating skyscrapers, serving both as clothes rails, accessory displays, and shoe displays. Small accessories are sold in 7 cm perspex balls. Coloured sprouts are springing up from a poodle of poisonous chemical residue, to form product displays.

LEVI'S BB Barcelona Summer

Project Name: LEVI'S BB Barcelona Summer **Designer:** Jump Studio **Location:** : Barcelona, Spain
Photographer: Go Sugimoto **Time:** 2007

This is another stand for the fashion fair Bread & Butter in Barcelona. Here the designers were asked to maintain the overall creative platform of 'The Night' but create something antithetical to the previous design. The brief was: 'Extremes and Everything In-Between'. This was to tap into particular product stories with the blackest of black washes to the whitest of white jeans.

The inspiration came from the Pantone reference cards where a colour range is demonstrated from one end of the spectrum to the other. They chose the colours of the Night, from the luminous white of the moon through to the blackest of blues for the deep, dark night sky. Rather than create the secretive, discovered spaces of the previous stand, here they created 360° open views of the stand from the centrally located bar, itself circular and lit, symbolizing the moon, with the product stories radiating out from this element on laser precise strips of colour.

Forum Duisburg

Project Name: Forum Duisburg   **Designer:** Chapman Taylor Architects
Location: Duisburg Germany   **Photographer:** Chapman Taylor Architects   **Time:** 2008

Forum Duisburg is an inner-city regeneration project located in the heart of Duisburg. The team worked with T+T Design to deliver the new, successful retail environment. The numerous pedestrian accesses linking the Forum with the surrounding streets play an important part in integrating the development to the existing urban grain. The malls are designed as individual buildings to create a continuation of the urban fabric and specifically the pedestrian street.

The 106,000-square-metre development offers 1,200 parking spaces, a direct underground railway link, a children's day care centre and a range of services for people with restricted mobility. It also includes 57,000 square metres of retail space spread across four levels and comprising 90 retailers, making it the largest inner-city retail project in North Rhine-Westphalia.

One of the principal anchor stores of Forum Duisburg is a new five-level Karstadt department store with an attractive landscaped roof garden. Spacious voids at all levels allow generous views between the four retail floors and create an open environment with squares, arcades and terraces. A harmonious, naturally-lit interior combines brick and stone walls with wood, brick and natural stone flooring.

As a part of the art programme, a specially designed 65-metre-high sculpture, 'Goldene Leiter' (Golden Ladder) connects all levels of the Forum and projects 54 metres above street level, protruding 35 metres through the glass roof to create a new, distinctive landmark on the city skyline. The ladder was made from 32 tonnes of steel that were then covered with 24-carat gold leaf.

Forum Duisburg is the first retail project in mainland Europe to be awarded a BREEAM 'Very Good' rating for its impressive sustainable features. The building materials used are prevalent throughout the region. A block heating unit allows power, heat and refrigeration to be generated on the spot, reducing average total energy consumption by at least 25 percent compared to that of similar shopping centres. The 10,000 square metres lawn roof above the department store was installed to improve the microclimate of the surrounding area.

Sexta Avenida

Project Name: Sexta Avenida   **Designer:** Chapman Taylor Architects   **Location:** Madrid Spain
Photographer: Chapman Taylor Architects   **Time:** 2006

Situated 13 km from the centre of Madrid in a prime location, this retail centre has been refurbished by Chapman Taylor Architects. Natural lighting through a new ceiling arrangement creates a brighter interior. Customer flows are improved and vertical circulation is added around a new meeting area. Floors, balustrades and other details are simple and contemporary, using good-quality materials.

Celebrity Solstice

Project Name: Celebrity Solstice   **Designer:** 5+design project team   **Location:** Los Angeles, USA
Time: 2008

Celebrity Solstice, part of Celebrity's Solstice-class fleet and the first of four vessels, has an exceptional range of guest-inspired services and amenities. Inspired by world-class resorts, Solstice offers its 2,850 guests the highest level of luxury, comfort and choices within the most stylish and varied public spaces at sea. 5+design drew on the inspiration of world-class resorts to assist Royal Caribbean in transitioning from a brand concept to a physical reality, creating a luxury product on the sea that will rival most land-based resorts.

As part of the Solstice design team, 5+design was responsible for planning the retail armature – the main spine of the ship, which includes the Fortunes Casino, Tasting's Bar, Art Gallery and the retail spaces of this next-generation ship. The Fortunes Casino was designed to evoke the luxury and grandeur of Europe's finest gaming resorts in a warm contemporary architectural language. It features a huge elliptical table gaming salon, as well as an exciting array of slot machines and other automated games of chance. Fortunes' elegant lounge with its luminous etched glass bar and rosette-coffered, gold-leafed ceiling offers both players and spectators a stake in the action.

The Art Gallery was inspired by light, transparency and interaction. Works of art are suspended on movable glass panels that open onto the deck 5 Galleria Shops and Tasting's Bar, a wonderful wine and aperitif venue. The Gallery also forms a balcony overlook to the boulevard shops below on deck 4. It is flooded with light coming from portside windows opposite the balcony. The unique and flexible design allows the gallery to be reconfigured for special events and presentations. Guests can easily meander through the space to the adjacent shops or enjoy a glass of wine while browsing the artwork, or relax on the casual seating at the balcony overlooking the boulevard shops and artwork.

The open and spacious design displays the wide variety of shopping and entertainment opportunities that can be enjoyed with new discoveries at every visit. This ship offers an upscale cruising experience with fine dining, exceptional personalized service and a great attention to detail throughout.

Gourmet

Project Name: Gourmet **Designer:** HEAD Architecture and Design Limited **Location:** Hong Kong China **Time:** 2005

This 15,000-square-foot food hall is situated in the basement of Causeway Bay's Lee Garden fashion district. The design fully utilises the dramatic impact of a five-storey sunlit atrium to illuminate the central part of the new store. This is given over to five individually designed concession 'pods', located in front of five equally spaced structural columns.

The rest of the store has been carefully planned to create a flowing but logical shopping experience in calm neutral colours, with an additional 'food street'. The 'food street' offers a variety of international lunchtime meals. This long refrigerated display counter snakes around the outer wall of the shopping centre and presents a variety of food. Taking this French fine dining theme, all departmental signage were in bilingual English and French.

By facing the preparation areas toward the customer, a better staff/customer relationship is created. The planning strategy promotes interaction, displays hygiene and shows culinary artistry.

A combination of ambient and focused lighting balances the functional and aesthetic requirements of the store. Spotlighting is focused over displays, while a variety of different light effects light the overall space.

Only Glass

Project Name: Only Glass   **Designer:** Robert Majkut Design studio   **Location:** Poznan, Poland
Photographer: Maciej Frydrysiak   **Time:** 2006

The place is, most obviously, made almost entirely out of glass (around 70% of the surface). Glass walls, glass ceilings, glass floors, glass staircases, glass railings and glass furniture – they all exemplify what a multi-functional material glass of all shapes and sizes is, that it can be used in a variety of surprising applications and combinations, and last but not least, that it not only an elegant, but also a pleasant material. The initial project constituted a basis for verification of the ideas and real possibilities, just before establishing the design of the Place Standards which for the designer, investor and contractor is a tool helping to create subsequent places of this kind. It denotes the only-glass trademark identity, its projects and development plans, localization and functional assumptions, materials used, shapes and finishing touches, and it serves the purpose of a consequent process of identity creation.
In order to consequently and consciously promote the only-glass trademark a sizeable Corporate Identity has been invented. Thanks to this, all the forms of the sign visible for the receiver are used in accordance with earlier specified standards as far as colours and typography are concerned. Promotional material and office stationery, or the signage inside the studio and on the elevation of the factory, have been designed according to specified patterns and requirements with moderate aesthetics dominated by yellow and black colours supplemented with grayish and violet hues.

Rocawear Mobile RocPopShop

Project Name: Rocawear Mobile RocPopShop   **Designer:** d-ash design   **Location:** Mobile unit, various locations   **Photographer:** Frank Oudeman   **Time:** 2008

When rapper Jay-Z wanted to launch his new premium apparel line for his Rocawear brand, d-ash design developed a mobile lounge and retail shop within a 53-foot tractor-trailer (1000 square feet). The concept was to create a Jay-Z inspired lounge and shop that would bring his new apparel line directly to his customers.

Supporting the mobile theme, display racks were designed as travel trunks, covered in patent leather and lined in suede. Plush materials and fabrics were utilized throughout the mobile unit to offer a luxurious shopping experience.

The mobile shop will travel around the country in 2009 and pop up at concerts, sporting events and in city centers. Customers will be able to hang out, shop and listen to music.

This is a new paradigm for shopping. It is both a store and a lounge. It has no permanent location. Tuesday it can be in Philadelphia and Wednesday it can be in Boston. The shop is a mobile marketing/brand experience.

SENSORA

Project Name: SENSORA   Designer: Design Clarity   Location: Sydney, Australia
Photographer: Design Clarity   Time: 2009

At Sensora there is a focus on service, indulgence and ultimate luxury. With a series of individual beauty treatment rooms, discreet 'microzones' for fast-turnaround mini facials, a 'skinbar' for product dabbling and makeovers, a comfortable communal hairstyling area and bespoke retail product display zones, Sensora offers the complete package. The store environment is sleek and minimal, restrained and sensual — answering the brief for the creation of an evocative space for sensory retailing.

Inspired by the science of skincare, Design Clarity created a distinct brand mark for Sensora reflecting the molecular makeup of skin cells. This logo device has been manipulated into a fragmented pattern and used as a recurring motif throughout the interior in blonde timber screening devices, sculptural wall pieces, mirrored panels, three-dimensional ceiling planes and subtle light features. The built environment and graphics have a consistent thread, which continues through the custom-made packaging concepts, uniform design, ticketing and even product shelf talkers. The shopfront design extends this scattered fractal pattern to the store façade across the frameless glass, inviting and intriguing customers to enter under a portal of pure white vitrified ceramic mosaic tiles.

Finishes have been selected to reflect a natural minimal aesthetic, American Oak flooring, white leather, mirror, low VOC paints, and white solid surface joinery. White on white walls and gloss on matt reflective signage elements add another layer of subtle texture to the interior and reinforce the Sensora brand. The day spa layout covers two adjacent retail tenancies and is set out at a 45-degree angle creating a more dynamic sense of space and allowing the display units and half height merchandise walls to face the customer on approach.

Design Clarity partnered with the Sensora directors and together delivered a unique, pure example of sensory experiential retailing.

UHA Mikakuto

Project Name: UHA Mikakuto   **Designer:** GLAMOROUS co.,Ltd   **Location:** Shanghai, China
Photographer: Nacasa & Partners, Inc.   **Time:** 2008

The client, UHA Mikakuto Co., Ltd., a famous long-established sweets manufacture in Japan, established its first flag shop in Shanghai, located at a popular streets' intersection.

The shop doubling as showroom has a dominating presence with the continuous huge shades above the showcases and the custom-made lighting stands covered with two-colour crystals which have been designed and are based on candies and chocolates.

While these striking lighting stands catch passengers' eyes, the classical wooden moldings dyed in chocolate colour successfully soften the whole space, being well-balanced.

The custom-made lighting fixtures above the long marble table by the window, generating different rhythm to the space, enhance their presence at night looking like floating in the air. Simple coloration of the interior flatters colourful sweets packages.

O2

A four-way pitch held in April this year led to the agency being selected to partner with the company to reposition its store network, supporting its "Connected World" strategy. Decidedly moving away from being a "phone shop" to being a platform for total connectivity, the new concept is set to truly evolve the format of retailing communication devices. The intangibility of O2's content and services will be core to the store of the future.

Central to the new store design is the creation of a newly appointed O2 Guru in each store. A futuristic bar starts in the window and sweeps around to form a service area in which the O2 Guru can operate to the side of the store. The window display aims to bring the tangible benefits of being on O2 to life rather than the technology itself. Customers will be able to seek technical help from the O2 Guru on products or services or simply to discover what's new or planned to be launched.

The strategy to create a complete "connected world experience" is brought alive by the physical layout of the product ranges. Phones and technology are displayed on bespoke pieces of furniture rather than the standard approach of using wall bays. Devices are laid out on fixtures to tell complete stories, with phones connected to the best accessories on the market, including headphones, printers and speakers. All products are live to encourage customer interaction and to discover the world of O2.

The store environment seamlessly links the worlds of the contemporary home and future technology without alienating the everyday customer. Contemporary concrete floor tiles and dark timber flooring are used to define different zones within the store. Overhead, the unique ceiling features sinuous interlocking blades, reflecting the form of sound waves.

At the back of the store, is the "lounge" area. Relaxed and inviting furniture positioned around a coffee table faces a huge 65" interactive touch-screen which will show product demonstrations, gaming, video clips from O2 and from sponsored sports events. Timber flooring, textured wall-covering and lampshades bring warmth to the environment and adds to the homely feel. The lounge area will also provide a space for O2's "It's Your Community" presentations where grants are presented to local community groups.

Lefel – The Whispering World

Project Name: Lefel – The Whispering World   **Designer:** Crea International   **Location:** Italy
Time: 2008

The new Lefel store intends to be a place for souls where a free and adventurous spirit, sometimes eccentric, puts the most significant objects of its wandering, travel by travel. It is a place where words, sounds, scents, past and future meet and where the objects tell stories and talk to people who have chosen them. It is a mutable and essential place where mysterious boxes, as transparent and light as thoughts at times, or as sturdy as wood other times, pick together objects that whisper little, big stories to the people who are able to listen to them.

Camilla Croce, design director explains the Lefel concept: "Stongly believing that style is secondary to sentiments in order to make our surroundings more human and ethic, I thought myself how I could create an affective relationship between customers and spaces they interact with. Just because it's that precise link which pushes us to come back shopping to the same place it was given birth in. Everybody, me included, has an old wooden box at home. Full of "black and white" keepsakes such as photos, letters, postcards and experiences where we can dip into for hours."

Lefel is a dream container where anyone can listen to enchanting stories told by a free and adventurous spirit — a spirit who collected and shares them with kindhearted people who believe in affective connections with everyday life objects.

Nike Airmax 360 Exhibition

Project Name: Nike Airmax 360 Exhibition   **Designer:** Mark Lintott , Chia Yen ,Alison Yang
Location: Taipei, China   **Photographer:** Marc Gerritsen   **Time:** 2007

Nike invited MLD to design a promotional space for the launch their new "Airmax 360" sports sneakers. The event took place on the ground floor at the newly opened flagship Eslite Bookstore in Shin-Yi District of downtown Taipei.

The theme of this new product presentation is related to "Walking on the Air", where the light-weight and transparent structure of the shoes was the main promotional focus. With this in mind, MLD designed a space defined by screens made of semi-transparent diaphanous cloth instead of hard surfaces or walls in a conventional sense. Behind the two sides of these fabric walls, a series of predecessors of "Airmax 360" sneakers representing the shoes' history were displayed in translucent acrylic display cases seemingly floating on air. Each case was lit by bundled strands of optical-fiber cables dropped from the ceiling. Visible through the fabrics, the essence of such a display resembles the light-weight and transparent feature of the product's structure.

In the centre the main focus of the installation was a group of 6 transparent acrylic globes hung only by optical-fiber cables which also provided the light source for each shoe. The latest "Airmax 360" sneakers were exhibited inside these acrylic spheres seemingly floating in space.

Kymyka shoes and bags, Maastricht

Project Name: Kymyka shoes and bags, Maastricht Kymyka   **Designer:** Maurice Mentjens Design, Holtum   **Location:** Maastricht, the Netherlands   **Photographer:** Arjen Schmitz   **Time:** 2009

Two patches of stainless steel rods, perched on top of which are artistic shoes, like colourful butterflies; an all-in-one wall unit of cupboards surrounding the space, intriguing and stylish — these are the signature style of Maurice Mentjens, responsible for the interior design of this exclusive shoe shop in Maastricht.

The shop space covers the ground floor of two city residences, the wall between which has been broken through, with a mirror-image floor plan. The houses were built at the beginning of the last century. Authentic original elements still in place include the plasterwork ceilings and two chimneys. One building still has the original windows; the other building was fitted with a large, low-silled display shop front in the 1970s.

Mentjens used the vertical lines of the premises as the basis for the structure of the design. The column that has replaced the partition wall stands exactly on the intersection of the floor plan. The steel supporting beam has been covered from floor to ceiling with mirrors. From this point, you can see the entire shop space through the mirrors. The two chimneys can be used as mirrors for customers trying on shoes. Since only the bottom 90 cm are covered in mirrors, these heavy structural features seem to float in space.

The space is entirely enclosed by low, multi-functional console tables. All the shop functions are contained in these: storage space and display cases, as well as cut-out seats and technical facilities such as the meter cupboard and heating. Only the sales counter itself protrudes into the space like a peninsula.

Another regular set of beams has been placed above the wooden console tables, a kind of minimalist wall frame forming the transition to the neo-baroque plasterwork that decorates both ceilings. These beams also embrace the room, and — through their linear simplicity — keep the irregular shape of the floor plan together, as it were. It is a surprisingly powerful design element that also has a functional side. The beams run right along the windows as well and make ideal display shelves for smaller items such as shoes and bags. The walls, ceiling and beams have been painted in the same colour and thus create a tranquil atmosphere.

Offspring Camden

Project Name: Offspring Camden   **Designer:** Shaun Fernandes, Sarah Williams
Location: London UK   **Photographer:** Mark York Photography   **Time:** 2008

Too many retailers slavishly try to reflect the culture of young people, witness the plethora of over-urbanised spaces, exposed brick, distressed leather sofas and graffiti.

Given the culture Offspring has always been a drive to innovate and a passion for the product; the inspiration for the design came from a need to reflect this culture, rather than slavishly following trends.

The approach has been to create a highly charged technologic landscape where nature is encapsulated in a technological playground of grass imbedded benches, cast resin trees snaking through the space and where the product is displayed on a swathe of polycarbonate 'blades' lining the perimeters of the shop. To change the pace where the product moves from footwear to apparel, they have created a system based on the language of an Air fix kit, with product replacing the model itself.

Sabateria Sant Josep

Project Name: Sabateria Sant Josep   **Designer:** Joan Casals Pañella / CSLS arquitectes
Location: Barcelona, Spain   **Photographer:** Eugeni Pons   **Time:** 2010

The client that came from a long generation of shop assistants, had some shops but he didn't feel identified with none of the shops. He needed a different place; he wanted to personalise his sale's style, his life's philosophy and survive like that to the competence. He acquired a new business with a main goal: substituting the old business and moving to the new one when it would be finished.

The new business has two different parts: the first one which is narrower and deeper gives access from the exterior of the shop; the second one is wider inside and the exitsting programs could be laid out (warehouse on the ground floor and in the upper floor, out from the intervention zone, the services).

The design is about unifying the two spaces to suggest a continuous trajectory through the programs of the shop. Talking about analogy, they understand space as an empty bottle. If the bottle's limit was what the content contains and the content in this case were the shoes, the only solution would be solving the container's limit.

The designers suggested a furniture-partition programme that would be able to transform into function the product that the client sells and the position where it's situated; it should be able to show, contain and transform the visual perception homogenizing the space. The shapes are intertwined to improve the product's vision and they just exist some inflection points to save constructive exisiting elements. Above all, the limit becomes an interior topography that has different meanings and it's able to contain the lightning, the air conditiong, the sound and of course the shoes. It is at the same time container and content.

The Eyecare Company

Project Name: The Eyecare Company   **Designer:** Design Clarity   **Location:** Sydney, Australia
Photographer: Design Clarity   **Time:** 2006

The Eyecare Company makes a bold statement on George Street, Sydney's flagship thoroughfare, and the concept demonstrates just how effective colour and pattern can be. The heritage listed site limited the treatment to the exterior of the building and challenged the designers to grab the attention of passers-by from within. The building's structure and location was capitalised with the injection of dynamic colour and graphics, providing theeyecarecompany massive exposure. The large-scale existing interior entry bulkhead also provided the perfect canvas for the store's strong new branding concept.

The store's prominent location in the heart of the CBD called for a design solution that was distinctive but with a professional edge. It was clear from the beginning that colour and a dynamic graphic identity would play an integral role in helping catch the attention of workers as they moved through the hustle and bustle of a busy city.

The design team began the project by looking optical illusions and was drawn to Op art of the 1960s. The designers agreed that the playful nature of this movement and its art was appealing, and the preoccupation with using pattern to create illusions proved instrumental when designing the logo for the project. As a result, the circle became a repeating motif that was used in different ways to direct the eye by framing the view.

The store's entrance is a dramatic interplay of colour and form and the large feature displays combined with the mobile trolleys reflect a sense of movement. Moreover, the circular merchandising units along the Jamison Street façade are presented at different heights directing the eye along a waveform. In addition, much of the joinery uses circular cut out viewing windows to display the glasses, creating a strong focal point.

FeiLiu Fine Jewellery

Project Name: FeiLiu Fine Jewellery   **Designer:** LISPACE   **Location:** Beijing, China
Photographer: LISPACE   **Time:** 2009

FeiLiu Fine Jewellery is a British high-end jewelry brand; recently opened in Beijing Blue Harbor Solana shop is the brand's first exclusive jewelry store in Asia, offering customised services. FeiLiu Fine Jewellery's jewelry design has a strong sense of space, and the designers fully extended such features to the store's interior design.

The initial orientation of the store design is to break the traditional way, to introduce the concept of Gallery experience. The main space is a showcase of different sizes, highlighting both the product and a sense of display sequence. Interior colours reflect a neutral fashion. Dark brown is adopted, and the brand's main colour purple is used for the background colour and the logo. Interior lighting design does not emphasise decorative function; they remain focused on products. Some showcases are equipped with luminous lamps, with auxiliary lighting throughout the space. The space of the store, the overall design and the lighting contribute to create the gallery atmosphere, so that guests, when purchasing the jewelry, would at the same time experience the "Jewelry Museum" atmosphere.

FeiLiu Fine Jewellery is small and exquisite. The cleverly divided display areas include precious metals, silver display area, cuffs display area, showing wear areas, VIP custom room, dressing rooms, and a rational allocation of office space of 150 square metres.

The jewelry store design, in a limited space to meet the functional needs of the space's exaggerated shape and style of the brand's jewelry design, is a successful experiment for a commercial space design.

Couronne

Project Name: Couronne   **Designer:** GLAMOROUS co.,ltd   **Location:** Tokyo, Japan
Photographer: Nacasa & Partners, Inc.   **Time:** 2007

The shop is located on the ground floor of a building designed by Tadao Ando in a peaceful quiet neighborhood and they sell very selected iconic watches from antique to cutting edge of the world. When you come in the shop, you will be overwhelmed by the beautiful copper colouration such as numerous wood beads hanging from the high ceiling.

The elegant showcases are surrounded with warm atmosphere from the natural materials such as wood beads and flooring, which successfully flatters the gorgeous watch selection. The central column has mirrors to broaden the space visually and enhance visual attractions. The luxurious continuous chandeliers standing on the copper-colour carpet also enhances the beauty of brilliant watches. The VIP room has artworks collected by the owner and classy furniture like an exclusive art gallery.

VAID Ginza

Project Name: VAID Ginza   **Designer:** GLAMOROUS co.,ltd   **Location:** Tokyo, Japan
Photographer: Nacasa & Partners, Inc   **Time:** March, 2007

Italy has a traditional craftsmanship of jewelry working. VAID, one of the best jewelry brand for its famous handmade chain, was established in 1929 in Rome, Italy. Their hand-rolled and hand-knitted chains with fine subtlety and delicacy are especially acclaimed by famous jewelry shops throughout the world.

GLAMOROUS received the offer from Samantha Thavasa Japan Limited to deign the shop with respects for such a traditional brand image. The principal designer, Yasumichi Morita, designed the shop as it would lead the branding image of "VAID". Based on the concept of "glamour and luxury", he produced the glamorous space, hanging the copper brown chains in wavy pattern with the lighting effect to introduce luxurious VAID's famous "handmade chains".

It is not easy to create the active air into the shop with the solo specific material; however, he took advantage of the texture of copper brown chains, giving theme a feeling of floating with lighting effect so that all chains look like dancing in the air in luxury. He believes that these dramatic chains will provide every customer great anticipations of high jewelries to be seen.

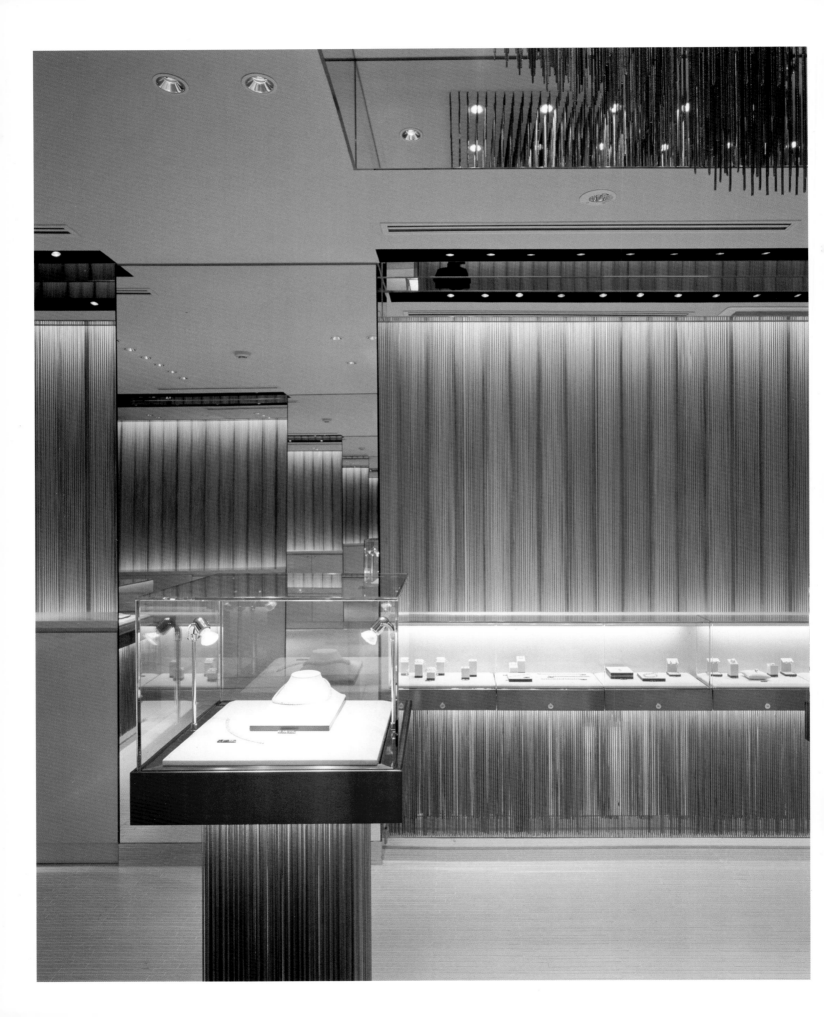

Index

Project: Murmuri Hotel
Design: Kelly Hoppen

Project: Hotel Sezz
Design: Shahé Kalaidjian, Christophe Pillet

Project: The George Hotel
Design: synergy hamburg

Project: Villa Florence Hotel
Design: sfa design

Project: JW Marriott Hotel Hong Kong
Design: JW Marriott Hotel Hong Kong

Project: Hotel Pirámides Narvarte
Design: DIN interiorismo, Aurelio Vázquez Durán

Project: Mövenpick Airport Hotel
Design: Matteo Thun & Partners

Project: The Library
Design: Tirawan Songsawat

Project: X2 Koh Samui
Design: Be Gray Limited

CULTURE

Project: Thurles Arts Centre and Library
Design: McCullough Mulvin Architects

Project: A.E. Smith High School Library
Design: Atelier Pagnamenta Torriani

Project: Wagner Middle School Library
Design: Atelier Pagnamenta Torriani

Project: Ps 11r Primary School Library
Design: Atelier Pagnamenta Torriani

Project: The Danish Jewish Museum
Design: Tomrerfirma Gert Fort A/S

Project: Museum
Design: JSª

Project: New Acropolis Museum
Design: Bernard Tschumi Architects

Project: The Art Institute of Chicago — The Modern Wing, Chicago
Design: Renzo Piano Building Workshop, Paris, France

Project: The Arts of Asia Gallery, Auckland
Design: Catherine Stormont, Nicole Pfoser, Gustavo Thiermann

Project: That's Opera
Design: Atelier Brueckner GmbH

Project: Bachhaus Eisenach
Design: Penkhues Architekten, Kassel

Project: Multikino Szczecin
Design: Robert Majkut Design studio

Project: Blue Room Theatre at Chesapeake
Design: Elliott+Associates Architects

Project: Ordrup School
Design: Bosch & Fjord

Project: Medical Faculty, University of Groningen
Design: RAU

FITNESS CENTRE

Project: Chesapeake Fitness Centre, East Addition
Design: Elliott + Associates Architects

Project: 14 Street Y Renovation
Design: Studio ST Architects

Project: Y+ Yoga Centre
Design: Lyndon Neri and Rossana Hu

EXHIBITION

Project: Breaking New Ground
Design: Jutta Friedrichs, Ben Houge

Project: Butterflies + Plants
Design: Reich + Petch Design International

Project: Fuji Xerox Epicenters
Design: Geyer Pty Ltd

Project: Stylecraft Showroom
Design: Geyer Pty Ltd

Project: Bernhardt Design Showroom
Design: Lauren Rottet, Kelie Mayfield, Christopher Evans

Project: BRANCH in Changchun
Design: Keiichiro SAKO, Yoshimasa TSUTSUMI / SAKO Architects

Project: FlatFlat in Harajuku
Design: Keiichiro SAKO, Yuichiro IMAFUKU / SAKO Architects

Project: homeculture
Design: Franken Architekten

Project: GRAFTWORLD — Exhibition in the Aedes Gallery
Design: Graftlab

Project: Moonraker
Design: Lam Cham Yuen & Lee Ming Yan, Olivia

Project: Internorm Flagshipstore
Design: ISA STEIN Studio

Project: Heaven
Design: Capella Garcia Arquitectura

STORE

Project: Tesla Store
Design: CCS Arhictecture

Project: ProNature
Design: Joey Ho / Joey Ho Design Ltd

Project: Healthy Life Natural Health Food Store
Design: Design Clarity

Project: Barbie Shanghai
Design: Slade Architecture

Project: WEEKDAY MALMÖ
Design: Electric Dreams

Project: Monki Stockholm
Design: Electric Dreams

Project: MONKI 1: Forgotten Forest
Design: Electric Dreams

Project: LEVI'S BB Barcelona Summer
Design: Jump Studio

Project: Forum Duisburg
Design: Chapman Taylor Architects

Project: Sexta Avenida
Design: Chapman Taylor Architects

Project: Celebrity Solstice
Design: 5+design project team

Project: Gourmet
Design: HEAD Architecture and Design Limited

Project: Only Glass
Design: Robert Majkut Design studio

Project: Rocawear Mobile RocPopShop
Design: d-ash design

Project: SENSORA
Design: Design Clarity

Project: UHA Mikakuto
Design: GLAMOROUS co., Ltd

Project: O2
Design: JHP

Project: Lefel—The Whispering World
Design: Crea International

Project: Nike Airmax 360 Exhibition
Design: Mark Lintott, Chia Yen, Alison Yang

Project: Kymyka shoes and bags, Maastricht
Design: Maurice Mentjens Design, Holtum

Project: Offspring Camden
Design: Shaun Fernandes, Sarah Williams

Project: Sabateria Sant Josep
Design: Joan Casals Pañella / CSLS arquitectes

Project: The Eyecare Company
Design: Design Clarity

Project: FeiLiu Fine Jewellery
Design: LISPACE

Project: Couronne
Design: GLAMOROUS co., ltd

Project: VAID Ginza
Design: GLAMOROUS co., ltd